PASTA

SUMMER • WINTER

GRACE PARISI

Photography by

MELANIE ACEVEDO

QUILL

WILLIAM MORROW AND COMPANY

NEW YORK

Library of Congress Cataloging-in-Publication Data
Parisi, Grace.
Summer / winter pasta / Grace Parisi.
p.   cm.
ISBN 0-688-15213-9
1. Cookery (Pasta)   I. Title.
TX809. M17P34   1997
641.8'22--dc21

97-6248
CIP

ISBN: 0-688-15213-9

Editor: DEBORAH MINTCHEFF
Designer: SUSI OBERHELMAN
Assistant Editor: SARAH STEWART
Assistant Designer: AYAKO HOSONO
Food Stylist: KEVIN CRAFTS
Prop Stylist: ROBYN GLASER

First Edition

1   2   3   4   5   6   7   8   9   10

PRODUCED BY SMALLWOOD & STEWART, INC., NEW YORK CITY

PRINTED IN SINGAPORE

introduction

4

conversion
chart

57

SOUPS

6

WINTER PASTA
CONTENTS

SIMPLE
MEALS

15

index

58

SAVORY
SUPPERS

27

BAKED
PASTAS

43

PASTA

WINTER

INTRODUCTION

What could be more comforting on a chilly evening than rigatoni with tomato meat sauce, its cheese hot and bubbling; a steaming bowl of home-made minestrone with toasted pastina; or a hearty lamb ragu scented with cinnamon and cumin and served over tagliatelle?

What follows are my favorite pasta dishes for cold weather, the robust fare we all yearn for. You'll find warming soups with escarole and beans; creamy cheese sauces and a rich carbonara to replace the light tomato sauces of summer; baked pastas instead of summer salads; and a glorious array of winter vegetables, from pumpkin, squash, and cauli-flower, to broccoli, cabbage, and crisp licorice-scented fennel. Pasta is one of our best-loved comfort foods, and these are dishes guaranteed to warm you even on the coldest winter's day.

CHANGING SEASONS: HOW TO USE THIS BOOK

When you feel like moving on to summer dishes, just flip the book over and you'll find a whole new set of recipes tailored to warm-weather dining. Each half is a mini book unto itself, complete with its own page numbers and index.

WINTER
PASTA

MINESTRONE WITH TOASTED PASTINA

¼ cup olive oil

2 carrots, cut into 1-x-¼-inch sticks

1 large onion, thinly sliced

2 large garlic cloves, minced

1 (28-ounce) can whole tomatoes, drained, seeded & chopped, juice reserved

2 tablespoons tomato paste

2 fresh thyme sprigs

1 bay leaf

Pinch of sugar

8 cups chicken broth, preferably homemade (p. 11)

½ pound green beans, trimmed & cut into 1-inch pieces

½ cup pastina

1 (15-ounce) can cannelini beans, drained & rinsed

1 small bunch broccoli, separated into 1-inch florets & stems coarsely chopped

½ small head cauliflower, separated into 1-inch florets

2 small zucchini, cut into 1-inch-thick pieces

Salt & freshly ground pepper

Freshly grated Parmesan cheese

TOASTING THE PASTINA GIVES IT A RICH NUTTY QUALITY THAT ADDS ANOTHER DIMENSION TO THIS CLASSIC ITALIAN VEGETABLE SOUP. I PREFER USING A RICHLY FLAVORED HOMEMADE CHICKEN BROTH HERE, SINCE MANY VEGETABLES ARE NOT AT THEIR PEAK OF FLAVOR AT THIS TIME OF YEAR.

In a large pot, heat 2 tablespoons of the oil over medium heat. Add the carrots, onion, and garlic and cook, stirring, for 4 minutes, or until softened. Add the tomatoes and their juice, the tomato paste, thyme, bay leaf, sugar, and broth and bring to a boil over medium-high heat. Reduce the heat to medium-low, partially cover, and simmer for 20 minutes, or until the carrots are crisp-tender. Add the green beans to the pot and cook for 5 minutes longer, or until crisp-tender.

Meanwhile, in a small skillet, heat the remaining 2 tablespoons oil over medium-low heat. Add the pastina and cook, stirring constantly, for 3 to 4 minutes, or until golden.

Add the pastina, cannelini beans, broccoli, cauliflower, and zucchini to the soup and season with salt and pepper. Cover and simmer for about 10 minutes, or until all the vegetables are tender.

To serve, ladle the minestrone into deep soup bowls and pass the Parmesan separately.

ESCAROLE-BEAN SOUP WITH TOMATO OIL

Serves 6

CREAMY WHITE BEANS AND TINY TUBE-SHAPED PASTA ARE COMBINED WITH ESCAROLE AND SMOKY BACON IN THIS HEARTY MAIN-COURSE SOUP. A DRIZZLE OF HOT-PEPPER-AND-TOMATO-INFUSED OIL ADDS DEPTH OF FLAVOR.

In a large pot, combine the beans, bouquet garni, and broth and bring to a boil over high heat. Reduce the heat to low, partially cover, and simmer for 1½ to 2 hours, or until the beans are soft but not mushy.

Meanwhile, prepare the spicy tomato oil: In a small skillet, combine the oil, tomato paste, garlic, and red pepper flakes. Cook, stirring, over medium-high heat for 8 minutes, or until the tomato paste looks sandy. Press through a strainer set over a bowl, season with salt, and set aside.

Remove the bouquet garni and discard. Put 2 cups of the cooked beans and 1 cup of the broth into a food processor and process until smooth. Stir the puree into the soup. Measure the soup. If it equals more than 5 cups, boil until reduced to 5 cups; if it measures less than 5 cups, add water to equal 5 cups. Season with salt and pepper and keep warm.

Cook the tubettini following the basic method (page 13), until al dente. Drain well and add to the soup.

Cook the bacon in a large skillet until crisp. Drain on paper towels then add to the soup. Increase the heat under the skillet to high, add the escarole and garlic and cook, stirring, for 1 minute, or until the escarole is wilted. Stir into the soup, season with salt and pepper, and simmer for 5 minutes. Ladle into bowls and top each with a swirl of spicy tomato oil.

1 cup dried navy or great northern beans, soaked overnight in cold water to cover, then drained & rinsed

bouquet garni (10 fresh parsley sprigs, 5 fresh thyme sprigs, 2 bay leaves & 1 fresh rosemary sprig tied with kitchen string)

8 cups chicken broth, preferably homemade (p. 11)

SPICY TOMATO OIL

3 tablespoons extra-virgin olive oil

2 tablespoons tomato paste

1 garlic clove, minced

½ teaspoon crushed red pepper flakes

Salt

Salt & freshly ground pepper

½ cup tubettini

4 slices good-quality bacon, cut into ¾-inch-pieces

2 small heads escarole, trimmed, cut crosswise into 1-inch-wide strips & washed

1 large garlic clove, thinly sliced

PASTA LENDICHE

Serves 4 to 6

MORE OF A THICK AND HEARTY STEW
THAN A SOUP, THIS COMFORTING DISH OF PASTA AND LENTILS
IS A COMPLETE MEAL IN ITSELF. IF YOU PREFER
IT SOUPIER, STIR IN SOME CHICKEN BROTH AT THE END.

In a large pot, cook the bacon over medium heat, stirring, until crisp and browned. Using a slotted spoon, transfer to a small bowl and set aside.

Pour off all but 3 tablespoons of the fat from the pot and return to medium heat. Add the carrots, onion, celery, and garlic and cook, stirring occasionally, for 10 minutes, or until softened. Stir in the lentils, tomatoes and their juice, the tomato paste, bouquet garni, bacon, and water, and bring to a boil over high heat. Reduce the heat to medium-low and cook, covered, for about 35 minutes, or until the lentils are tender but not mushy. (Lentils can cook in as little time as 30 minutes or as long as 1 hour, depending on their freshness.)

If the garlic cloves are still whole, mash with a fork against the side of the pot. Discard the bouquet garni. Add the tubetti, salt, and pepper and cook for about 8 minutes, or until the pasta is al dente. Add the escarole and cook, stirring, for 2 minutes, or until just wilted.

Meanwhile, in a small skillet, heat the oil and fennel seeds in a small skillet over high heat, stirring constantly, for 2 minutes, or until golden and fragrant. Transfer to a small dish.

Ladle the soup into deep bowls and top with the fennel seeds and oil.

¼ pound slab bacon,
   cut into ¼-inch dice

2 medium-size carrots,
   cut into ½-inch dice

1 medium-size onion,
   cut into ½-inch dice

1 celery stalk, cut into
   ½-inch dice

4 large garlic cloves, lightly
   smashed

1¼ cups lentils, picked over
   & rinsed

1 (14-ounce) can diced tomatoes,
   undrained

1 tablespoon tomato paste

bouquet garni (3 fresh flat-leaf
   parsley sprigs, 3 fresh
   thyme sprigs & 1 bay leaf
   tied with kitchen string)

7 cups cold water

½ cup tubetti or ditali

2 teaspoons salt

¼ teaspoon freshly ground pepper

1 small head escarole or 1 bunch
   spinach, trimmed, washed
   & coarsely chopped

1 tablespoon olive oil

¼ teaspoon fennel seeds

WINTER VEGETABLE SOUP WITH PESTO

PESTO

½ cup packed fresh basil leaves

2 tablespoons extra-virgin
    olive oil

1 teaspoon unsalted butter,
    at room temperature

Twelve ¼-inch-thick slices
    French bread

¼ cup olive oil

1 large garlic clove, halved

3 medium-size carrots,
    cut into 1-inch chunks

2 parsnips, peeled & cut into
    1-inch chunks

1 leek, cut into ¼-inch-thick
    slices & washed well

1 small buttercup or butternut
    squash (about 2 pounds),
    peeled, halved, seeded & cut
    into 1-inch chunks

4 fresh thyme sprigs

2 bay leaves

⅛ teaspoon freshly grated nutmeg

2 teaspoons salt

¼ teaspoon freshly ground
    pepper

THE SWEET, DELICATE FLAVORS OF CARROTS, PARSNIPS, AND BUTTERCUP SQUASH BLEND TO MAKE THIS SOUP ABSOLUTELY SUBLIME. BUTTERCUP SQUASH, ALSO KNOWN AS KABOCHA SQUASH, HAS SWEET DRY FLESH, WITH A TASTE AND TEXTURE SOMEWHERE BETWEEN THAT OF SWEET POTATOES AND BUTTERNUT SQUASH.

Preheat the oven to 350°F.

Prepare the pesto: In a blender or food processor, process the basil, pulsing, until finely chopped. Add the oil and the butter and process until smooth. Transfer to a small bowl and set aside.

Put the bread slices on a baking sheet and brush on both sides with 2 tablespoons of the oil. Toast in the oven for 8 minutes, or until golden and crisp. Rub the bread on one side only with the garlic and set aside.

In a large pot, heat the remaining 2 tablespoons oil over medium heat. Add the carrots and parsnips; cook for 8 minutes, stirring, or until browned. Add the leek and cook for 3 minutes, or until soft. Raise the heat to high, add the squash and cook for 2 minutes. Add the thyme, bay leaves, nutmeg, salt, pepper, and broth and bring to a boil. Reduce the heat to medium-low, partially cover, and cook for 18 to 20 minutes, or until the vegetables are just tender. Discard the thyme sprigs and bay leaves.

Meanwhile, cook the pasta following the basic method (page 13),

until barely al dente. Drain. Add the pasta to the soup, partially cover and cook for 3 minutes, or until the pasta is al dente.

To serve, ladle the soup into shallow soup plates and top each with a small dollop of pesto and 2 slices garlic bread.

6 cups Chicken Broth
(recipe follows)

½ cup farfalline

CHICKEN BROTH

Makes 2 quarts

In a large pot, combine all of the ingredients and bring to a boil over high heat. Reduce the heat to medium and simmer for 20 minutes, skimming the froth that rises to the surface. Reduce the heat to low, partially cover, and simmer for 2 hours, or until rich-tasting.

Pour the broth through a fine-mesh strainer into a large bowl. Return to the pot and boil until reduced to 8 cups.

Note: To make Rich Chicken Broth, boil over high heat until reduced to 4 cups.

6 pounds chicken backs,
legs and/or wings

2 medium-size onions, quartered

3 celery stalks, coarsely chopped

2 medium-size carrots,
coarsely chopped

12 cups cold water

FISH CHOWDER WITH CAPELLINI & ROUILLE

Serves 6

ROUILLE

3 tablespoons mayonnaise

2 tablespoons extra-virgin
   olive oil

1 teaspoon tomato paste

1 teaspoon fresh lemon juice

½ teaspoon paprika

¼ teaspoon ground red pepper

¼ cup extra-virgin olive oil

2 garlic cloves, smashed

3 large shallots, thinly sliced

1 (14-ounce) can diced tomatoes,
   drained & juice reserved

1 tablespoon tomato paste

Four ¼-inch-thick slices lemon,
   quartered

¼ teaspoon each dried thyme &
   crushed red pepper flakes

Fish stock (recipe follows)

Salt & freshly ground pepper

4 ounces capellini, broken into
   2-inch lengths

1½ pounds firm-fleshed white
   fish, skinned, boned & cut
   into 1½-inch pieces

½ cup assorted olives, pitted

TENDER PIECES OF FISH, OLIVES, LEMON, AND TOMATOES COME TOGETHER IN THIS HEARTY SOUP. A SPICY ROUILLE ADDS JUST THE RIGHT AMOUNT OF HEAT AND RICHNESS. CHOOSE FIRM-FLESHED WHITE FISH THAT CAN STAND UP TO ASSERTIVE FLAVORS, SUCH AS HALIBUT, SNAPPER, COD, MONKFISH, OR TRIGGERFISH.

Prepare the rouille: Combine all the ingredients in a small bowl, whisking until blended. Set aside.

In a large pot, heat 3 tablespoons of the oil over medium heat. Add the garlic and cook, stirring, for 3 minutes, or until golden. Add the shallots and cook about 3 minutes, or until softened. Stir in the tomatoes and tomato paste and cook, stirring, until the juices have thickened slightly. Add the lemon, thyme, red pepper flakes, fish stock, and the reserved tomato juice. Bring to a boil over medium-high heat. Reduce the heat to medium-low, partially cover, and simmer for 20 minutes. Mash the garlic cloves with a fork against the side of the pot and season the soup with salt and pepper.

In a small skillet, heat the remaining 1 tablespoon oil over high heat. Add the capellini and cook, stirring, for 2 minutes, or until golden.

Stir the pasta into the soup and cook, covered, for 8 to 10 minutes, or until al dente. Add the fish and olives and cook for about 3 minutes, or until the fish flakes easily.

To serve, ladle the soup into bowls and top with some of the rouille.

BASIC PASTA COOKING METHOD

In a large pot, bring 4 quarts of cold water to a boil over high heat; add 2 tablespoons salt. Add the pasta and cook, stirring occasionally to prevent the pasta from sticking, until al dente. (Use the cooking time indicated on the pasta box as a guide since it varies, depending on the brand and type of pasta.) To test for doneness, cut through a piece of pasta. When the pasta is al dente, it is considered firm to the bite—it should not be hard. Drain the pasta by pouring it into a colander; shake out the excess water. The pasta should not be rinsed unless specified in the recipe.

FISH STOCK

Makes 1½ quarts

In a large pot, heat the oil over high heat. Add the fish bones and scraps and cook, stirring occasionally, for 2 minutes, or until opaque. Add the carrot, onion, parsley, lemon, thyme, and peppercorns, and cook, for about 5 minutes, or until the vegetables are almost tender. Add the vermouth and cook until the liquid has evaporated. Add the water and bring to a boil over high heat, skimming off any froth that rises to the surface. Reduce the heat to medium, partially cover, and cook for 30 minutes.

Pour the stock through a fine-mesh strainer into a large bowl. Measure the broth: If necessary, add water to equal 6 cups, or return to the pot and gently boil until reduced to 6 cups.

1 tablespoon olive oil

3 pounds non-oily fish
bones & scraps

1 medium-size carrot, chopped

1 medium-size onion, quartered

10 fresh flat-leaf parsley sprigs

½ lemon, cut into chunks

¼ teaspoon dried thyme

10 whole black peppercorns

¼ cup dry vermouth

10 cups cold water

MUSSEL CHOWDER WITH CHORIZO

½ pound chorizo, halved lengthwise & cut crosswise into
¼-inch-thick slices

3 pounds mussels, debearded
& scrubbed well

1 large fennel bulb, trimmed &
cut into ¼-inch dice, tough
outer leaves, stalks &
feathery tops reserved

¾ cup each dry white wine
& cold water

2 tablespoons olive oil

1 medium-size onion, cut into
¼-inch dice

2 large garlic cloves, thinly sliced

Three strips orange zest

¼ teaspoon saffron threads

1 (28-ounce) can whole tomatoes,
drained & chopped, juice
reserved

1 tablespoon tomato paste

1 red bell pepper, roasted
(Summer, p. 22), peeled,
cored, seeded &
cut into ½-inch dice

Pinch of sugar

Salt & freshly ground pepper

½ cup stelline

THE CLEAN FLAVORS OF SAFFRON, ORANGE, AND FENNEL
ACCENT THIS SATISFYING CHOWDER. SUBSTITUTE ANDOUILLE
SAUSAGE FOR THE CHORIZO IF YOU LIKE.

In a medium-size skillet, cook the chorizo over medium-high heat for 3 minutes, or until browned. Transfer to a small plate and set aside.

In a large pot, combine the mussels, the reserved fennel stalks and outer leaves, the wine, and water. Cover and cook over high heat for 8 minutes, or until the mussels open; discard any that don't open. Remove the mussels from their shells and put into a medium-size bowl, discarding the shells. Pour the cooking liquid through a fine-mesh strainer into a large glass measuring cup and add water to equal 3 cups. Slowly pour the liquid into a bowl, leaving any grit behind.

Wash the pot. Add the oil and place over medium heat. Add the diced fennel, onion, and garlic and cook, stirring, for 6 minutes, or until softened. Add the orange zest and saffron and cook for 1 minute. Add the tomatoes, tomato paste, bell pepper, and sugar and stir until blended. Add the reserved tomato juice and mussel liquid and bring to a simmer. Partially cover the pot and simmer for 20 minutes, or until the vegetables are tender. Season with salt and pepper; discard the orange peel.

Meanwhile, cook the stelline following the basic method (page 13), until barely al dente. Drain.

Add the pasta, mussels, and chorizo to the chowder. Cover and cook for about 3 minutes. Season with salt and pepper. To serve, ladle into shallow soup bowls and garnish with the reserved fennel tops.

GOLDEN
ORECCHIETTE

THIS IS A PASTA DISH THAT SICILIANS OFTEN
ENJOY. THE COMBINATION OF SWEET AND SAVORY INGREDIENTS,
INFLUENCED BY THE CUISINES OF AFRICA
AND THE MIDDLE EAST, MAKE IT UNUSUAL AND SATISFYING.

¼ cup golden raisins

2 tablespoons cold water

2 tablespoons Cognac

1 small head cauliflower,
cut into ¾-inch florets

12 ounces orecchiette or farfalle

2 tablespoons unsalted butter

2 tablespoons olive oil

1 large onion, thinly sliced

1 teaspoon sugar

3 anchovy fillets, chopped

½ cup chicken broth, preferably
homemade (p. 11)

Salt & freshly ground pepper

¼ cup pine nuts, toasted

Freshly grated Parmesan cheese,
for serving

Preheat the oven to 350°F.

Combine the raisins, water, and Cognac in a small bowl and set aside. Bring a large pot of generously salted water to a boil over high heat. Add the cauliflower and cook for 5 minutes, or until tender. Using a slotted spoon, transfer the cauliflower to a medium-size bowl and cover to keep warm. Cook the orecchiette in the cauliflower water, following the basic method (page 13), until al dente. Drain well, transfer to a large bowl, and cover.

In a large deep skillet, heat the butter and oil over medium heat. Add the onion and sugar and cook for 6 minutes, stirring occasionally, or until the onion is softened and just golden. Add the anchovies and stir until combined. Add the cauliflower and cook, stirring occasionally, for 3 minutes, or until golden. Add the broth and raisins, along with the soaking liquid, and season lightly with salt and pepper. Cook for 3 to 4 minutes, or until the liquid is reduced by half. Use a wooden spoon to mash half of the cauliflower against the side of the skillet. Reduce the heat to low, add the pasta, and cook, stirring, for 3 minutes, or until some of the liquid is absorbed. Stir in the pine nuts and serve immediately in deep bowls. Pass the Parmesan on the side.

PAPPARDELLE WITH WILD MUSHROOMS

Serves 4 to 6

1 pound pappardelle

1 tablespoon extra-virgin
olive oil

¼ pound thinly sliced pancetta,
coarsely chopped

1 pound wild mushrooms, such
as shiitakes, porcinis, or
chanterelles, stems trimmed,
briefly rinsed & cut into
¼-inch-thick slices

1 small head escarole, trimmed,
cut into 1-inch-wide strips
& washed

2 large garlic cloves, minced

Salt & freshly ground pepper

1 cup chicken broth, preferably
homemade (p.11)

1 teaspoon cornstarch dissolved
in 2 tablespoons cold water

THIS DELICIOUS PASTA DISH IS RICH AND
HEARTY—PERFECT FOR A CHILLY EVENING. IT CAN BE
PREPARED IN LITTLE MORE THAN THE
TIME IT TAKES TO BRING PASTA WATER TO A BOIL.

Cook the pappardelle following the basic method (page 13), until al dente. Drain well and cover to keep warm.

Meanwhile, in a large skillet, heat the oil over medium-high heat. Add the pancetta and cook, stirring often, for 2 minutes, or until crisp and browned. Using a slotted spoon, transfer the pancetta to a small bowl. Add the mushrooms to the skillet and cook, tossing occasionally, for 6 to 8 minutes, or until softened and beginning to brown. Transfer to a large plate and set aside.

Add the escarole, with any water clinging to the leaves, and the garlic to the skillet. Cook over medium-high heat, tossing often, for about 2 minutes, or until the escarole is wilted. Return the mushrooms to the skillet and season with salt and pepper. Add the chicken broth and bring to a boil. Briefly whisk the cornstarch mixture and add to the skillet. Cook, stirring, for about 1 minute, or until the sauce simmers and is slightly thickened.

Add the pasta and cook, tossing just until heated through. Add the pancetta, toss, and transfer to large shallow bowls.

SPAGHETTI ALLA CARBONARA

4 large eggs, at room temperature

½ cup freshly grated Parmesan cheese, plus additional, for serving

¼ cup mascarpone cheese, crème fraîche, or heavy cream

¼ cup chopped fresh flat-leaf parsley

Freshly ground pepper

6 ounces pancetta or 12 slices bacon, cut into ½-inch pieces

12 ounces spaghetti

Salt

THERE ARE MANY VARIATIONS OF THIS CLASSIC DISH. SOME CONTAIN BACON, EGGS, AND CHEESE, OTHERS BROWN BUTTER AND CREAM, AND OTHERS WINE. NO MATTER WHAT THE EXACT INGREDIENTS, THE DISH IS ALWAYS RICH AND LUSCIOUS AND NOT FOR THE DIET-CONSCIOUS. THE HEAT OF THE PASTA COOKS THE EGGS, CREATING THE CREAMY SAUCE, SO IT IS IMPORTANT TO HAVE YOUR EGGS AT ROOM TEMPERATURE AND TO WORK QUICKLY.

In a large bowl, combine the eggs, Parmesan, mascarpone, and parsley, season generously with pepper, and set near the stove.

In a large skillet, cook the pancetta over medium-high heat until crisp and browned. Using a slotted spoon, transfer the pancetta to a small bowl and set aside. Pour off all but 1 tablespoon of the fat from the skillet; set the skillet aside.

Cook the pasta following the basic method (page 13), until al dente. Drain the pasta, reserving ¼ cup of the pasta water.

Transfer the pasta to the skillet and return to high heat. Cook for 1 minute, tossing to coat the pasta. Transfer to a large heated serving bowl. Working quickly, add the egg mixture and 2 tablespoons of the reserved pasta water, tossing to combine. Add the pancetta, season with salt and pepper, and toss again. Serve immediately in heated bowls and pass additional Parmesan on the side.

FETTUCCINE WITH BACON & BRIE

Serves 4

THIS IS COMFORT FOOD. THIN RIBBONS OF
CABBAGE, CARROTS, AND ONIONS ARE TOSSED WITH
FETTUCCINE, CRISP BACON, AND
BRIE. A HINT OF CARAWAY AND SHERRY VINEGAR ADDS
RICHNESS TO THIS HEARTY WINTER PASTA.

1 large carrot, cut into
2-x-¼-inch sticks

½ small head green or red
cabbage, tough ribs
removed & leaves cut into
½-inch-wide strips

8 slices bacon, cut into
¾-inch pieces

1 large onion, thinly sliced

¼ teaspoon caraway seeds

¼ cup chicken broth

¼ cup cold water

2 tablespoons sherry vinegar

Salt & freshly ground pepper

4 ounces Brie cheese, rind
removed & cut into
½-inch dice

12 ounces fettuccine

1 tablespoon chopped fresh
flat-leaf parsley

Bring a large saucepan of water to a boil over high heat. Add the carrot and cook for 3 minutes, or until crisp-tender. Using a slotted spoon, transfer to a small bowl. Add the cabbage to the saucepan and cook for 5 minutes, or until tender. Drain well and set aside.

Cook the bacon in a large nonstick skillet over medium heat until crisp and browned. Transfer to a small bowl and set aside. Pour off all but 2 tablespoons of the fat from the skillet and return the skillet to medium heat. Add the onion, carrot, cabbage, and caraway seeds and cook, stirring occasionally, for 10 minutes, or until the vegetables are tender. Add the broth, water, and vinegar, and season with salt and pepper. Cover and cook for 10 minutes, or until the vegetables are very tender. Add the Brie and stir until melted. Remove from the heat and keep warm.

Meanwhile, cook the pasta following the basic method (page 13), until al dente. Drain well, reserving ¼ cup of the pasta water.

Add the pasta and parsley to the sauce, and toss, adding the reserved pasta water, 1 tablespoon at a time, if the mixture seems dry. Transfer to a serving bowl, sprinkle with the bacon, and serve immediately.

TORTELLINI WITH CRISP SAGE

Serves 4

THIS IS A SIMPLE YET RICHLY SATISFYING
DISH THAT REQUIRES ONLY A MINIMUM OF INGREDIENTS.
TRY MAKING YOUR OWN CRÈME FRAÎCHE—
IT'S SURPRISINGLY EASY TO DO. STIR ONE TEASPOON
CULTURED BUTTERMILK INTO ONE CUP
HEAVY CREAM AND LET SIT, COVERED, AT ROOM TEMPERATURE,
FOR TWENTY-FOUR HOURS. REFRIGERATE
THE THICKENED CRÈME FRAÎCHE, WHICH WILL THICKEN
EVEN FURTHER AS IT CHILLS.

½ cup vegetable oil

20 large fresh sage leaves, patted dry

Salt

⅔ cup thinly sliced shallots

1 pound cheese-, wild mushroom-, or pumpkin-filled tortellini, agnolotti, or cappeletti

½ cup crème fraîche

Freshly ground white pepper

In a medium-size skillet, heat the oil over medium heat until it shimmers. Fry the sage leaves, in batches, for about 30 seconds, or until crisp. Transfer the sage to a paper towel–lined plate and sprinkle with salt.

Add the shallots to the skillet and cook over medium heat, stirring, for 4 minutes, or until softened. Transfer the shallots to a serving bowl.

Cook the pasta following the basic method (page 13), until al dente. Drain well.

Crumble half the sage leaves. Add the pasta and crème fraîche to the shallots. Season with salt and pepper, and add the crumbled sage, tossing until mixed well. Garnish with the whole sage leaves and serve immediately.

VERMICELLI WITH BROCCOLI RABE

Serves 4 to 6

1 pound broccoli rabe, stems trimmed, thick stems peeled & leaves coarsely chopped

1 tablespoon olive oil

2 garlic cloves, thinly sliced

⅛ teaspoon crushed red pepper flakes, or more to taste

Salt

¾ pound sweet Italian sausages (preferably pork-and-fennel), removed from casings & broken into chunks

¼ cup dry white wine

½ cup chicken broth, preferably homemade (page 11)

12 ounces vermicelli

¼ cup freshly grated Parmesan cheese

BROCCOLI RABE, SOMEWHAT OF AN ACQUIRED TASTE, IS MADE LESS BITTER WHEN IT IS BRIEFLY BLANCHED BEFORE BEING SAUTEED. HERE, IT IS PAIRED WITH ITALIAN SAUSAGE, RED PEPPER FLAKES, AND LOTS OF FRESHLY GRATED PARMESAN.

Bring a large saucepan of water to a boil over high heat. Add the broccoli rabe and cook for 2 minutes, or until wilted and bright green. Drain well.

In a large deep skillet, heat the oil over medium-high heat. Add the broccoli rabe, garlic, red pepper flakes, and season with salt. Cook, stirring occasionally, for 5 minutes, or until the garlic is golden (watch to make sure the garlic doesn't burn) and the broccoli rabe is just beginning to brown around the edges. Transfer to a large bowl. Add the sausage to the skillet and cook, stirring occasionally, for 6 minutes, or until browned. Add the wine and cook until evaporated, scraping to loosen any browned bits in the bottom of the pan. Add the broth and cook until reduced to ¼ cup. Return the broccoli rabe to the skillet. Season with salt, toss, and cook for about 2 minutes or until heated through.

Meanwhile, cook the pasta following the basic method (page 13), until al dente. Drain well.

Add the pasta to the skillet and toss until well combined. Transfer to a serving bowl, sprinkle with the Parmesan, and serve.

BUCATINI WITH TUNA SAUCE

Serves 4

THIS INCREDIBLY QUICK CLASSIC SAUCE
IS FULL OF FLAVOR: TANGY TOMATOES, TUNA, ANCHOVIES, AND
OF COURSE, GARLIC. BUCATINI, A THIN
HOLLOW SPAGHETTI WITH A LOT OF BODY, STANDS UP
WELL TO THE FULL FLAVOR OF THE SAUCE.

2 tablespoons extra-virgin olive oil

3 anchovy fillets

2 large garlic cloves, lightly smashed

2 cups canned diced tomatoes, undrained

$\frac{1}{8}$ teaspoon crushed red pepper flakes, or to taste

Pinch of sugar

Pinch of salt

1 (6-ounce) can oil-packed Italian tuna, drained & lightly flaked

12 ounces bucatini

In a medium-size saucepan, heat the oil over medium-high heat. Add the anchovies and garlic and cook, stirring, for 3 minutes, or until the garlic is golden and the anchovies are broken up. Raise the heat to high and add the tomatoes and their juice, the red pepper flakes, sugar, and salt. Cook, stirring, for about 5 minutes, or until the juices have reduced. Remove the garlic, mash it with a fork, and return it to the sauce. (Discard the garlic if you prefer a milder sauce.) Add the tuna and cover to keep warm.

Meanwhile, cook the pasta following the basic method (page 13), until al dente. Drain well. Toss the pasta with the tuna sauce and serve immediately in deep bowls.

FUSILLI MARINARA WITH TWO RICOTTAS

Serves 4

2 tablespoons extra-virgin
  olive oil

1 large garlic clove, lightly
  smashed

1 (28-ounce) can diced tomatoes,
  undrained

¼ teaspoon sugar

½ teaspoon salt

⅛ teaspoon crushed red
  pepper flakes

⅔ cup ricotta cheese, at room
  temperature

12 ounces long fusilli

⅔ cup crumbled ricotta salata
  or feta cheese

WHEN I WAS A CHILD, MY MOTHER OFTEN PREPARED THIS SIMPLE YET SOPHISTICATED DISH WHEN TIME WAS A BIT TIGHT. WHEN WE WERE LUCKY ENOUGH TO FIND IT, RICOTTA SALATA—PRESSED, SALTED, AND AGED RICOTTA CHEESE—WAS SPRINKLED ON THE TOP.

In a medium-size saucepan, heat the oil over medium-high heat. Add the garlic and cook for about 2 minutes, or until golden and fragrant. Add the tomatoes, sugar, salt, and red pepper flakes and cook, stirring occasionally, for 15 to 18 minutes, or until the sauce has thickened. Using a fork, mash the garlic against the side of the saucepan.

Meanwhile, press the creamy ricotta through a fine-mesh strainer set over a large serving bowl.

Cook the pasta following the basic method (page 13), until al dente. Drain. Add the pasta to the serving bowl along with the tomato sauce, tossing until well combined. Sprinkle with the ricotta salata and serve.

PAPPARDELLE WITH CHICKEN LIVERS

¾ pound chicken livers, trimmed
    & cut into 1-inch pieces

½ cup ruby port

12 ounces pappardelle

1 tablespoon extra-virgin olive oil

1 tablespoon plus 1 teaspoon
    unsalted butter, at room
    temperature

Salt & freshly ground pepper

4 medium-size shallots, minced

⅔ cup chicken broth

1 teaspoon all-purpose flour

Chopped fresh tarragon,
    for garnish (optional)

> WHEN CHICKEN LIVERS ARE MARINATED IN PORT, THEY RETAIN JUST ENOUGH OF THE PORT'S FLAVOR AND SWEETNESS TO HELP THEM CARAMELIZE BEAUTIFULLY.

Combine the chicken livers and port in a medium-size bowl and let sit in the refrigerator for 30 minutes. Drain and pat dry, reserving the port.

Cook the pappardelle following the basic method (page 13), until al dente. Drain well, transfer to a large serving bowl, and keep warm.

Meanwhile, in a large skillet, heat the oil and 1 tablespoon of the butter over medium-high heat. When the foam subsides, season the livers with salt and pepper and add to the skillet. Cook, turning occasionally, for 3 minutes, or until browned and crusty on the outside but still pink in the middle. Transfer the livers to a small bowl and cover to keep warm.

Add the shallots to the skillet and cook over medium heat, stirring, for 4 minutes, or until softened. Add the reserved port and bring to a simmer, scraping to loosen any browned bits in the skillet. Cook until reduced to 2 tablespoons. Raise the heat to high, add the broth, and bring to a boil.

Using your fingers, blend the flour with the remaining 1 teaspoon butter until a paste forms. Add to the sauce, whisking constantly, until blended. Reduce the heat to medium and cook, stirring, for about 1 minute, or until the sauce thickens. Return the livers to the sauce, season with salt and pepper, and cook for 1 minute, or until heated through.

Pour the sauce over the pasta, sprinkle with the tarragon, and serve.

SPAGHETTI ALLA ARRABBIATA

EVERYONE HAS THEIR OWN IDEA ABOUT HOW
HOT AND SPICY ARRABBIATA SAUCE SHOULD BE. THE AMOUNT
OF RED PEPPER FLAKES IN MY VERSION IS JUST
ENOUGH TO ADD A SATISFYING AMOUNT OF HEAT WITHOUT
OVERWHELMING THE OTHER FLAVORS IN THE SAUCE.

8 slices bacon or ¼ pound sliced pancetta, finely diced

½ small onion, minced

1 large garlic clove, minced

¼ teaspoon crushed red pepper flakes

1 (28-ounce) can diced tomatoes, undrained

Pinch of sugar

Pinch of salt

12 ounces spaghetti

Freshly grated Pecorino Romano cheese, for serving

Heat a large saucepan over medium-high heat. Add the bacon, onion, and garlic and cook, stirring, for 5 minutes, or until the bacon just begins to turn pink. Add the red pepper flakes and cook until the bacon is just beginning to darken. Add the tomatoes and their juice, the sugar, and salt and bring to a boil. Reduce the heat to medium-low, partially cover, and simmer for 30 minutes, or until the sauce has thickened.

Meanwhile, cook the spaghetti following the basic method (page 13), until al dente. Drain well. Toss the pasta with the sauce. Serve in deep bowls with the Romano alongside.

RIGATONI WITH
FENNEL & TOMATOES

Serves 4

RIGATONI STANDS UP PERFECTLY TO THIS
CHUNKY WINTER VEGETABLE SAUCE WHICH IS ACCENTED BY
THE DELICATE FLAVORS OF ORANGE, FENNEL, AND BASIL.

2 tablespoons unsalted butter

2 tablespoons extra-virgin olive oil

1 large fennel bulb, trimmed & thinly sliced, feathery tops chopped

2 medium-size leeks, thinly sliced & washed well

2 large shallots, minced

¼ cup dry red wine

1 (28-ounce) can whole tomatoes, drained, chopped & juice reserved

1 large roasted red bell pepper (**Summer, p. 22**), peeled cored, seeded & cut into ¼-inch-wide strips

2 tablespoons capers, rinsed

1 tablespoon grated orange zest

1½ teaspoons sugar

1 teaspoon dried herbes de Provence*

Salt & freshly ground pepper

12 ounces rigatoni

2 tablespoons shredded fresh basil, for garnish

In a large saucepan, heat the butter and oil over medium-high heat. Add the sliced fennel and cook, stirring, for 10 minutes, or until softened. Add the leeks and shallots and cook for 3 minutes, or until softened. Stir in the wine and cook until most of the wine has evaporated, scraping to loosen any browned bits in the bottom of the pan. Add the tomatoes and their juice, the bell pepper, capers, orange zest, sugar, and herbes de Provence. Season with salt and pepper, reduce the heat to low, partially cover, and cook for 20 minutes, or until the sauce is slightly thickened. Remove from the heat and set aside.

Meanwhile, cook the rigatoni following the basic method (page 13), until al dente. Drain well.

To serve, toss the pasta with the sauce, divide among bowls, and garnish with the basil and chopped fennel tops.

*Herbes de Provence are available in specialty food stores.

PASTA WITH RAGU BOLOGNESE

¼ cup extra-virgin olive oil

1 large onion, cut into ¼-inch dice

1 each carrot & celery stalk, cut into ¼-inch dice

2 ounces sliced pancetta, cut into ¼-inch dice

½ pound each ground beef & veal

¼ pound ground pork

2 large garlic cloves, minced

¾ cup dry white wine

1 (28-ounce) can whole tomatoes, drained, seeded & chopped, juice reserved

1 cup Rich Chicken Broth (p. 11) or veal broth

½ teaspoon dried thyme

1 bay leaf

Freshly ground pepper

1 pound fettuccine or rigatoni

Salt

¼ cup heavy cream

2 tablespoons finely chopped fresh parsley

Freshly grated Parmesan cheese, for serving

IN EMILIA-ROMAGNA, WHERE RAGU IS A WEEKLY TRADITION, RAGU BOLOGNESE IS THE SAUCE OF CHOICE.

In a large heavy saucepan, heat 1 tablespoon of the oil over medium heat. Add the onion, carrot, celery, and pancetta and cook, stirring occasionally, for 6 to 8 minutes, or until the vegetables are softened but not browned. Transfer to a medium-size bowl and set aside.

Add the remaining 3 tablespoons oil to the saucepan and increase the heat to medium-high. Add the beef, veal, and pork and cook, breaking the meat into chunks, for 5 minutes, or until just firm but not cooked all the way through. Increase the heat to high, add the garlic and reserved vegetables, and cook for 1 minute. Add the wine and cook, stirring, until most of the liquid has evaporated. Add the tomatoes and their juice, the broth, thyme, bay leaf, and a generous pinch of pepper and bring to a boil. Reduce the heat to medium-low, partially cover, and cook for 1 hour, or until the sauce has thickened.

Meanwhile, cook the pasta following the basic method (page 13), until al dente. Drain and transfer to a large bowl. Season the sauce with salt and pepper. Stir in the cream and parsley and heat thoroughly; be sure not to allow the sauce to boil once the cream has been added. Pour the sauce over the pasta, toss well, and serve in deep bowls. Pass the Parmesan separately.

RIGATONI WITH TOMATO MEAT SAUCE

Serves 10 to 12

TEEMING WITH SAUSAGE, MEATBALLS, AND TENDER CHUNKS OF MEAT, THIS LONG-SIMMERED TOMATO SAUCE IS WELL WORTH THE EFFORT. SERVE IT OVER A STURDY PASTA SUCH AS RIGATONI OR PENNE WITH LOTS OF CRUSTY ITALIAN BREAD ALONGSIDE.

Prepare the tomato sauce: In a large Dutch oven, heat the oil over medium-high heat until it shimmers. Cook the veal and pork in batches, turning occasionally, for about 6 minutes, or until browned. Remove the meat as it browns to a platter. Add the sausages to the pot and cook, turning occasionally, for 8 minutes, or until golden. Transfer to the platter.

Pour off all but 1 tablespoon of the fat from the pot. Add the onion and garlic and cook, stirring, for 3 minutes, or until softened. Return all the meats to the pot, along with any juices that have accumulated, the water, tomatoes and their juice, the tomato puree, tomato paste, sugar, and bay leaves. Season lightly with salt and pepper. Reduce the heat to low, partially cover, and cook, stirring occasionally, for 1½ hours, or until the meat is very tender.

Meanwhile, prepare the meatballs: In a small skillet, heat the oil over medium heat. Add the onion and garlic and cook, stirring, for 3 minutes, or until softened. Add the thyme and rosemary and cook for 1 minute, or until fragrant. Transfer to a large bowl and cool slightly.

In a small bowl, soak the bread in the milk until soggy. Add the egg,

TOMATO SAUCE

2 tablespoons extra-virgin olive oil

1 pound each boneless lean veal & pork shoulder, cut into 1-inch cubes

1 pound sweet or hot Italian sausage, or a combination

1 large onion, finely chopped

4 large garlic cloves, minced

2 cups cold water

2 (28-ounce) cans whole tomatoes, drained & chopped, juice reserved

1 (28-ounce) can tomato puree

1 (6-ounce) can tomato paste

2 tablespoons sugar

3 bay leaves

Salt & freshly ground pepper

MEATBALLS

1 teaspoon olive oil

1 medium-size onion, minced

1 large garlic clove, minced

1 teaspoon dried thyme

½ teaspoon dried rosemary, crushed

3 slices firm white bread

¼ cup milk

1 large egg, beaten

2 tablespoons freshly grated
    Parmesan cheese

2 tablespoons chopped fresh
    flat-leaf parsley

1 teaspoon salt

½ teaspoon freshly ground
    pepper

½ pound each ground beef
    & veal

Vegetable oil for panfrying

¼ cup all-purpose flour

1½ pounds rigatoni, ziti,
    or penne

Freshly grated Parmesan cheese,
    for serving

Parmesan, parsley, salt, and pepper, stirring until well combined. Add the bread mixture, ground beef, and ground veal to the onions, mixing well. Divide into 12 portions, and using wet hands, roll into meatballs.

In a large skillet, heat ½ inch vegetable oil over medium-high heat. Put the flour on a plate. Dust the meatballs with the flour and add to the skillet. Cook, turning, for 3 minutes, or until browned on all sides. Using a slotted spoon, transfer the meatballs to the sauce, partially cover, and cook the sauce for 30 minutes longer.

Meanwhile, cook the pasta following the basic method (page 13), until al dente. Drain well and transfer to a large serving platter. Arrange the meats around the pasta and ladle some sauce on top. Serve with the remaining sauce and Parmesan on the side.

SEAFOOD & SAFFRON RISOTTO

1 pound littleneck clams or cockles, scrubbed well

1 pound small mussels, debearded & scrubbed well

¾ cup cold water

¾ cup dry white wine

2 garlic cloves, smashed

Pinch of saffron threads

½ pound medium-size shrimp, peeled & deveined

¼ pound cleaned baby squid, bodies cut into ¼-inch rings & tentacles left whole

1¼ cups orzo

1 tablespoon extra-virgin olive oil

1 medium-size carrot, finely chopped

1 celery stalk, finely chopped

3 large shallots, thinly sliced

3 tablespoons unsalted butter, at room temperature

2 tablespoons chopped fresh flat-leaf parsley

Salt & freshly ground pepper

ORZO, RICE-SHAPED PASTA, REPLACES ARBORIO RICE IN THIS "FAUX RISOTTO." IT'S IMPORTANT TO PARBOIL THE ORZO SEPARATELY TO PREVENT THE RISOTTO FROM BECOMING GLUEY.

Put the clams and mussels into a large deep skillet with a tight-fitting lid. Add the water, ½ cup of the wine, and the garlic. Cover and cook over high heat for 5 to 10 minutes, or until the clams and mussels open, transferring them to a bowl as they open; discard any that do not open. Pour the clam and mussel liquid through a paper towel–lined strainer into a large glass measuring cup. If needed, add water to equal 1¾ cups. Crumble in the saffron and set aside.

Cook the shrimp and squid in a medium-size saucepan of boiling water for 1 minute, or just until cooked through. Drain and set aside with the clams and mussels.

Cook the orzo in a medium-size saucepan of boiling salted water for 5 to 6 minutes, or until barely tender. Drain well and set aside. Wash the saucepan and dry well.

In the saucepan, heat the oil over medium-high heat. Add the carrot, celery, and shallots and cook, stirring occasionally, for 8 minutes, or until the vegetables are softened and just beginning to brown. Add the orzo and cook, stirring, for 1 minute. Add the remaining ¼ cup wine and cook, stirring constantly, for 1 minute, until the orzo has absorbed the wine. Reduce the heat to medium. Add about ⅓ of the saffron broth and cook, stirring constantly, until the broth has been absorbed. (The broth should simmer gently.) Continue cooking, adding the broth in 2 more additions, and allowing the orzo to absorb the broth before adding more, until the orzo is al dente. If all the broth is used before the orzo is tender, add a little hot water.

Stir in the seafood, butter, and parsley and season with salt and pepper. Cook, stirring gently, for 1 to 2 minutes, or until heated through. Serve immediately in large shallow soup plates.

SAVORY PAPPARDELLE WITH RABBIT

3 tablespoons olive oil

4 slices bacon, cut into ¼-inch-wide strips

1 (2½-pound) rabbit, cut into 8 pieces

Salt & freshly ground pepper

3 medium-size carrots, 1 finely chopped, 2 cut into 1-inch pieces

1 small onion, finely chopped

1 celery stalk, finely chopped

2 large garlic cloves, halved

2 tablespoons all-purpose flour

1 cup dry white wine

2 cups Rich Chicken Broth (p. 11) or veal broth

1 cup water

1 tablespoon tomato paste

½ teaspoon dried thyme

1 bay leaf

Pinch of sugar

12 small white boiling onions, halved

1 tablespoon unsalted butter

THIS CLASSIC TUSCAN DISH COMBINES TENDER STEWED RABBIT WITH WIDE NOODLES IN A RICH FLAVORFUL SAUCE—PERFECT WINTER FARE. RABBIT IS AVAILABLE FROZEN IN MANY SUPERMARKETS AND FRESH RABBIT CAN BE ORDERED FROM MOST BUTCHERS, WHO WILL BE MORE THAN HAPPY TO CUT IT UP FOR YOU.

In a large deep skillet, heat 2 tablespoons of the oil over medium-high heat. Add the bacon and cook until browned and crisp. Using a slotted spoon, transfer the bacon to a small bowl and set aside. Season the rabbit with salt and pepper and add to the skillet. Reduce the heat to medium and cook for 10 minutes, turning occasionally, or until browned and crusty on all sides. Transfer to a platter and set aside.

Add the finely chopped carrot, onion, celery, and garlic to the skillet and cook, stirring, for 5 minutes, or until softened and browned. Stir in the flour and cook for 1 minute. Add the wine and cook for about 2 minutes, or until the juices are thickened, scraping to loosen any browned bits in the bottom of the skillet. Return the rabbit to the skillet. Add the broth, water, tomato paste, thyme, bay leaf, and sugar and a pinch of salt, and bring to a boil over medium-high heat. Reduce the heat to medium-low, cover, and cook, stirring occasionally, for 1 hour, or until the rabbit is very tender and the sauce has thickened. Transfer the rabbit to a platter and cover to keep warm.

Meanwhile, steam the remaining carrots and the boiling onions in a steamer basket set into a large saucepan containing 1 inch boiling water for 7 minutes, or just until tender. Set aside.

Strain the sauce through a fine-mesh strainer set over a medium-size bowl, pressing on the solids with the back of a wooden spoon to extract as much of the sauce as possible. Wipe out the skillet and return the sauce to the skillet. Using your fingers, remove the rabbit meat from the bones and cut or shred into bite-size pieces. Add the rabbit to the sauce, season with salt and pepper, and cover to keep warm.

In a large skillet, heat 1½ teaspoons of the oil and 1½ teaspoons of the butter over medium-high heat. Add the steamed carrots and onions and cook for 6 minutes, or until browned and tender; add to the sauce. Increase the heat under the skillet to high and add the remaining 1½ teaspoons each oil and butter. Add the mushrooms and cook, stirring occasionally, for 6 minutes, or until softened and golden. Add to the sauce along with the bacon and cook over low heat for 5 minutes to allow the flavors to blend.

Meanwhile, cook the pasta following the basic method (page 13), until al dente. Drain well and transfer to a large serving bowl.

Pour the sauce over the pasta, toss gently to combine, and serve.

¾ **pound button mushrooms, stems trimmed, briefly rinsed & quartered**

12 ounces pappardelle

HEARTY LAMB RAGU

Serves 4 to 6

THE CUISINES OF SICILY AND NORTH AFRICA
WERE INSPIRATION FOR THIS FULL-FLAVORED RAGU. THE
CAREFUL BLENDING OF SPICES, HERBS, TOMATOES,
AND THE UNEXPECTED SWEETNESS OF GOLDEN RAISINS, MAKES
FOR AN APPEALING AND EXOTIC SAUCE.

- 2 tablespoons olive oil
- 1 pound boneless lean lamb shoulder, cut into ¾-inch chunks
- Salt & freshly ground pepper
- 1 medium-size onion, finely chopped
- 2 large garlic cloves, minced
- ½ teaspoon ground cumin
- ¼ teaspoon ground cinnamon
- ⅛ teaspoon ground allspice
- ⅛ teaspoon freshly grated nutmeg
- ½ cup dry red wine
- 2 tablespoons tomato paste
- 1 (14-ounce) can whole tomatoes, drained & chopped, juice reserved
- 1 cup beef broth
- 2 fresh thyme sprigs
- 1 teaspoon sugar
- 12 ounces tagliatelle or fettuccine
- 1 (15-ounce) can chickpeas, drained & rinsed
- ½ cup golden raisins, coarsely chopped
- ¼ cup crumbled ricotta salata

In a large deep skillet, heat the oil over medium-high heat. Lightly season the lamb with salt and pepper. Cook, in batches, for about 8 minutes, or until browned and crusty on all sides. Transfer to a medium-size bowl.

Add the onion and garlic to the skillet and cook, stirring, for 3 minutes, or until softened. Add the cumin, cinnamon, allspice, and nutmeg and cook, stirring constantly, for about 30 seconds. Stir in the wine and tomato paste and cook, stirring, for 1 minute, or until thickened, scraping to loosen any browned bits in the bottom of the skillet. Add the lamb, tomatoes and their juice, the broth, thyme, and sugar and bring to a boil. Reduce the heat to low, cover, and cook, stirring occasionally, for 1 hour, or until the lamb is very tender and the sauce has thickened.

Meanwhile, cook the pasta following the basic method (page 13), until al dente. Drain well. Add the chickpeas and raisins to the ragu and cook for 5 minutes longer to allow the flavors to blend. Discard the thyme sprigs and season with salt and pepper. Transfer to a large bowl and cover to keep warm. Divide the pasta evenly among large shallow soup plates, spoon the ragu over, and sprinkle with the ricotta salata. Serve hot.

VEAL & PORCINI MUSHROOM RAGU

2 pounds boneless lean veal shoulder, cut into ¼-inch chunks

Zest of 1 lemon (removed with a vegetable peeler)

1 large fresh rosemary sprig, broken into several pieces

Freshly ground pepper

¼ cup plus 1 tablespoon olive oil

½ cup dried porcini mushrooms (about 1 ounce)

1 cup boiling water

Salt

4 medium-size carrots, cut into ½-inch dice

1 medium-size onion, halved & thinly sliced

2 large garlic cloves, thinly sliced

2 tablespoons all-purpose flour

1½ cups dry white wine

1½ cups Rich Chicken Broth (p. 11) or veal broth

Pinch of Sugar

12 ounces penne or farfalle

1 tablespoon fresh lemon juice

1 tablespoon chopped fresh flat-leaf parsley

TENDER PIECES OF VEAL, SCENTED WITH FRESH ROSEMARY AND LEMON, ARE SLOWLY COOKED WITH PORCINI MUSHROOMS IN A RICH HOMEMADE CHICKEN BROTH. THE RICH EARTHY QUALITY OF THE DRIED PORCINI MUSHROOMS IS ACCENTED AND LIGHTENED BY THE ADDITION OF FRESH LEMON ZEST AND JUICE. THIS RAGU TASTES EVEN BETTER WHEN MADE A DAY AHEAD SO THE FLAVORS HAVE TIME TO DEVELOP.

In a medium-size bowl, combine the veal, lemon zest, rosemary, a generous pinch of pepper, and 2 tablespoons of the oil, tossing to coat the veal. Cover and marinate in the refrigerator for least 30 minutes or up to 2 hours.

Soak the porcini mushrooms in the boiling water in a small bowl for 20 minutes, or until softened. Pour through a small paper towel–lined strainer set over a small bowl. Chop the mushrooms and reserve the mushrooms and liquid separately.

In a large deep skillet, heat 1 tablespoon of the oil over high heat. Lightly season the veal with salt. Cook the veal along with the lemon zest and rosemary, in small batches, for 8 minutes, or until browned on all sides, adding the remaining 2 tablespoons oil as needed. Set the veal aside in a large bowl.

Reduce the heat to medium-low and add the carrots, onion, garlic, and porcini mushrooms. Cook, stirring, for 5 minutes, or until the vegetables are softened. Sprinkle the flour over the vegetables, tossing until

coated. Add the wine and cook, scraping to loosen any browned bits in the bottom of the skillet. Return the veal to the skillet, add the broth, the reserved mushroom liquid, the sugar, and a pinch of salt and pepper. Bring to a boil, then reduce the heat and simmer for 45 minutes, or until the veal is very tender and the sauce has thickened.

Meanwhile, cook the penne following the basic method (page 13), until al dente. Drain well, transfer to a large serving bowl, and cover to keep warm.

Remove and discard the rosemary sprigs from the ragu. Stir in the lemon juice and parsley, and spoon over the pasta, tossing to combine. Serve hot.

MACARONI AI QUATTRO FORMAGGI

EACH ONE OF THESE FOUR CHEESES—
PUNGENT, SWEET, SALTY, STRINGY, AND CREAMY—CONTRIBUTES
SOMETHING DISTINCTIVE TO THIS LUXURIOUS DISH.

- 2 tablespoons unsalted butter
- 1 medium-size onion, thinly sliced
- ½ teaspoon sugar
- 1 tablespoon all-purpose flour
- 1 cup milk
- Salt & freshly ground pepper
- ⅓ cup crumbled Gorgonzola cheese
- 8 ounces pennette
- ½ cup fine dried bread crumbs
- ¼ cup freshly grated Asiago cheese
- ½ cup diced mozzarella cheese (¼-inch)
- ½ cup diced Italian Fontina cheese (¼-inch)

In a large skillet, melt 1½ teaspoons of the butter over medium heat. Add the onion and sugar and cook, stirring, for 5 minutes, or until the onion is softened. Reduce the heat to medium-low and cook, stirring, for 10 minutes, or until the onion is lightly browned. Transfer to a small bowl.

In a small saucepan, melt 1 tablespoon of the butter over medium-high heat. Add the flour and cook, whisking, for 1 minute. Whisk in the milk and bring to a boil. Reduce the heat to medium and cook, whisking, for 2 to 3 minutes, or until thickened. Season with salt and pepper and stir in the Gorgonzola and caramelized onions. Set aside.

Preheat the oven to 400°F. Cook the pasta following the basic method (page 13), until al dente. Drain, reserving ¼ cup of the water.

Melt the remaining 1½ teaspoons butter in a small skillet; stir in the bread crumbs. Put into a small bowl; stir in 2 tablespoons of the Asiago.

Generously grease an 8-inch square baking dish and sprinkle 2 tablespoons of the bread crumb mixture over the bottom.

In a large bowl, combine the pasta, Gorgonzola sauce, mozzarella, Fontina, the remaining 2 tablespoons Asiago, and 3 tablespoons of the reserved pasta water. Pour into the prepared baking dish and sprinkle with the remaining bread crumb mixture. Bake for 20 minutes, or until bubbling and the top is golden. Let rest for about 5 minutes before serving.

WILD MUSHROOM & LEEK TIMBALE

¼ cup dried porcini mushrooms

¼ cup boiling water

8 ounces capellini

½ cup plus 2 tablespoons freshly grated Parmesan cheese

½ cup fine dried bread crumbs

3 tablespoons olive oil

Salt & freshly ground pepper

1 tablespoon unsalted butter

1 large leek, thinly sliced & washed well

1 pound portobello mushrooms, stems removed, briefly rinsed, black underside removed, halved & thinly sliced crosswise

¼ teaspoon dried thyme

1 cup heavy cream

2 large eggs, lightly beaten

½ cup grated Italian Fontina cheese

THIS IS JUST THE DISH FOR SPECIAL OCCASIONS. THE TIMBALE MAKES AN ELEGANT PRESENTATION— IDEAL IN SMALL PORTIONS AS A FIRST COURSE AND PERFECT AS A MEATLESS MAIN COURSE SERVED ALONGSIDE A COLORFUL BITTER GREENS SALAD DRESSED WITH A WARM BALSAMIC VINAIGRETTE.

Soak the porcini mushrooms in the boiling water in a small bowl for 20 minutes, or until softened. Pour through a small paper towel–lined strainer set over a small bowl. Reserve the mushrooms and liquid separately.

Meanwhile, cook the pasta following the basic method (page 13), until almost al dente. Drain well and rinse briefly under cold running water, until just barely warm. Drain well, transfer to a large bowl, cover, and set aside.

Preheat the oven to 425°F. Generously grease the bottom and sides of a 2-quart soufflé dish.

In a small bowl, combine 2 tablespoons of the Parmesan, the bread crumbs, 2 tablespoons of the oil, and salt and pepper to taste. Sprinkle half of the bread crumbs into the soufflé dish, turning the dish to coat the bottom and sides evenly. Reserve the remaining bread crumbs.

In a large skillet, heat the butter and the remaining 1 tablespoon oil over medium-high heat. Add the leek and cook, stirring, for 3 minutes, or until just softened. Add the portobellos, the porcini mushrooms, the reserved mushroom liquid, and the thyme and cook, stirring, for 8

minutes, or until the mushrooms are softened and browned. Transfer to a large plate and cool slightly, then add to the pasta and toss until combined.

In a medium-size bowl, combine the cream, eggs, the remaining ½ cup Parmesan, the Fontina, 1 teaspoon salt, and ¼ teaspoon pepper. Pour over the pasta and mix until well combined. Pour into the prepared dish and sprinkle with the reserved bread crumbs. Bake for 45 minutes, or until golden brown and set. Let rest for 10 minutes.

Place a large serving plate over the soufflé dish, invert, and carefully lift off the dish. Cut the timbale into wedges and serve.

WINTER LASAGNE

Serves 6 to 8

SUCCULENT EGGPLANT AND WILD MUSHROOMS
ADD A MEATINESS TO THIS VEGETARIAN LASAGNE. LOOK FOR
LONG SLENDER EGGPLANTS THAT WEIGH ABOUT
ONE POUND EACH. THEY TEND TO HAVE FEWER SEEDS THAN
THE ROUNDER, MORE BULBOUS VARIETIES.

TOMATO SAUCE

¼ cup olive oil

3 large garlic cloves, lightly smashed

2 (28-ounce) cans whole tomatoes, drained & chopped, juice reserved

1 cup cold water

3 tablespoons tomato paste

½ teaspoon sugar

1 teaspoon salt

¼ teaspoon freshly ground pepper

3 medium-size eggplants (about 1 pound each), peeled & cut into ½-inch-thick slices

2 tablespoons olive oil

Salt & freshly ground pepper

¾ pound wild mushrooms such as shiitakes, creminis & chanterelles, stems trimmed, briefly rinsed & thickly sliced

1 pound ricotta cheese, preferably fresh

Prepare the tomato sauce: In a large saucepan, heat the oil over medium heat. Add the garlic and cook, stirring occasionally, for 2 minutes, or until golden. Stir in the tomatoes and their juice, the water, tomato paste, sugar, salt, and pepper and bring to a boil over medium-high heat. Reduce the heat to low, partially cover, and simmer, stirring occasionally, for about 1 hour, or until thickened. Use a fork to mash the garlic cloves against the side of the saucepan. Set aside.

Meanwhile, preheat the oven to 425°F. Position the oven racks in the middle and lower third of the oven.

Place the eggplant in a single layer on a large baking sheet. Brush with 1 tablespoon of the oil and sprinkle with salt and pepper. In a 2-quart baking dish, toss the mushrooms with the remaining 1 tablespoon oil and season with salt and pepper. Roast the eggplant for about 30 minutes and the mushrooms for about 15 minutes, or until tender and browned, reversing the pans halfway through the baking time. Transfer the mushrooms to a medium-size bowl and cool slightly. Stir in the ricotta, ¼ cup of the Parmesan, the basil, thyme, and nutmeg, and season with salt and pepper.

While the vegetables are roasting, cook the lasagne noodles follow-

¼ cup plus 2 tablespoons
   freshly grated Parmesan
   cheese

½ cup chopped fresh basil

½ teaspoon dried thyme

¼ teaspoon freshly grated
   nutmeg

12 ounces lasagne noodles
   (about 15)

12 ounces mozzarella cheese,
   grated (about 3 cups)

ing the basic method (page 13), until al dente. Drain well and transfer to a large baking pan lined with waxed paper. Cool.

Reduce the oven temperature to 400°F. Lightly grease a 13-x-9-inch baking dish.

Cover the bottom of the baking dish with ½ cup of the tomato sauce. Place one third of the noodles over the sauce in an overlapping layer. Spread half of the ricotta mixture over the noodles, top with about 1 cup of the mozzarella, half of the eggplant slices, and 1½ cups of the tomato sauce. Continue layering, until all the ingredients are used. Sprinkle the remaining 2 tablespoons Parmesan over the top. Cover loosely with foil.

Bake for about 40 minutes, or until bubbling. Remove the foil and bake for about 20 minutes longer, or until the top is browned and crisp. Let rest for about 15 minutes before serving.

BAKED RIGATONI WITH SUN-DRIED TOMATOES

Serves 6

SMOKY HAM AND SUN-DRIED TOMATOES
ADD DEEP FLAVORS TO RIGATONI BAKED IN A MASCARPONE-
ENRICHED TOMATO SAUCE. THIS LUSCIOUS
DISH CAN BE MADE IN JUST ABOUT ONE HOUR, OR LESS
IF YOU HAVE THE SAUCE ON HAND.

12 ounces rigatoni

2½ cups marinara sauce, homemade (p. 24) or store-bought, or Arrabbiata Sauce (p. 27), heated

12 oil-packed sun-dried tomatoes, cut into ¼-inch-wide strips

½ pound smoked ham, cut into ½-inch dice

½ cup mascarpone cheese

Salt & freshly ground pepper

4 ounces mozzarella cheese, cut into ¼-inch dice (about 1 cup)

4 ounces Italian Fontina cheese, cut into ¼-inch dice (about 1 cup)

¼ cup freshly grated Parmesan cheese

Preheat the oven to 400°F. Grease a 13-x-9-inch baking dish.

Cook the pasta following the basic method (page 13), until al dente. Drain well, reserving ½ cup of the pasta water.

In a large bowl, combine the pasta, marinara sauce, sun-dried tomatoes, ham, mascarpone, and the reserved pasta water. Season with salt and pepper. Spread half of the pasta in an even layer in the prepared baking dish. Sprinkle with half of the mozzarella and half of the Fontina, and cover with the remaining pasta. Sprinkle with the remaining mozzarella and Fontina and top with the Parmesan.

Bake, uncovered, for 30 minutes, or until bubbling and crusty on top. Let rest for 10 minutes, then cut into squares and serve.

PAELLA
WITH FIDEO

½ pound chorizo, cut into
¼-inch-thick slices

1 pound sweet Italian sausages

2 cups cold water

¼ cup plus 1 tablespoon olive oil

1 (2½-pound) chicken, cut
into 8 pieces

Salt & freshly ground pepper

1 medium-size onion, finely diced

2 large garlic cloves, minced

12 ounces fideo in nests*

1½ cups diced ham (reserved
from Tomato-Ham Broth)

Tomato-Ham Broth
(recipe follows)

1 cup frozen baby peas, thawed

Lemon wedges, for garnish

*Fideo in nests is available in
ethnic markets and in some
supermarkets.

THIS PAELLA IS MADE WITH VERMICELLI
(FIDEO) THAT COME SHAPED IN NESTS. THE FIDEO IS LIGHTLY
CRISPED IN OIL THEN LAYERED WITH CHORIZO (SPICY
SAUSAGE), CHICKEN, ITALIAN SAUSAGE, AND TOMATO-HAM
BROTH TO CREATE A RICHLY FLAVORED MAIN DISH.

Heat a large heavy skillet over medium-high heat. Add the chorizo and cook, stirring, for 2 minutes, or until browned. Transfer the chorizo to a platter. Reduce the heat to medium, add the Italian sausages and cook, turning occasionally, for 12 minutes, or until browned. Cut each sausage into 3 pieces and transfer to the platter. Add 1 cup of the cold water to the skillet and simmer for 1 minute, scraping to loosen any browned bits in the bottom of the skillet. Pour into a large glass measuring cup.

Wipe out the skillet. Return the skillet to high heat and add 1 tablespoon of the oil. Season the chicken with salt and pepper, put into the skillet, skin side down, and cook, turning once or twice, for 8 to 10 minutes, or until browned and crusty. Transfer the chicken to the platter, set the skillet aside, and remove the skin from the breasts and thighs.

Place the skillet over medium heat. Add the onion and garlic and cook, stirring, for 4 minutes, or just until softened. Add the remaining 1 cup water and cook for 1 minute, scraping to loosen any browned bits in the bottom of the skillet. Add to the liquid in the glass measuring cup.

Wipe out the skillet and heat the remaining ¼ cup oil over medium heat. Cook the pasta nests, in batches, turning frequently, for 1 to 2 min-

utes, or until deep golden. Transfer the nests to a paper towel–lined tray.

Preheat the oven to 400°F.

Transfer the pasta nests to a 15-x-11-inch baking dish, arranging them in a single layer. Place the chicken thighs, legs, and wings, the chorizo, sausages, and ham on top. Pour the tomato broth and the reserved pan liquid over, cover tightly, and bake for 25 minutes.

Add the chicken breasts to the baking dish, cover tightly, and bake for 10 minutes longer, or until most of the liquid is absorbed and the chicken breasts are almost cooked through. Add the peas and cook for 5 minutes longer, or until the liquid is absorbed and the chicken is cooked through. Let the paella sit, covered, for at least 5 minutes before serving. Garnish with the lemon wedges just before serving.

1 smoked ham hock (about 1½ pounds)

1 (14-ounce) can diced tomatoes, undrained

1 bay leaf

2 large garlic cloves, crushed

8 cups cold water

2 teaspoons salt

½ teaspoon freshly ground pepper

TOMATO-HAM BROTH

Makes 1 quart

In a large saucepan, combine the ham hock, tomatoes, bay leaf, garlic, and water and bring to a boil over high heat. Partially cover, reduce the heat to medium-low, and simmer for 1 hour, or until the meat is tender.

Transfer the ham hock to a cutting board, remove the meat, and cut into ½-inch dice. Reserve the diced ham for the paella. Skim the fat from the broth and season with the salt and pepper.

CHICKEN & PASTA TIMBALLO

Serves 6

SHAPED LIKE A DRUM (ITS NAME IN ITALIAN), A TIMBALLO IS AN ELEGANT PIE THAT IS USUALLY RESERVED FOR SPECIAL OCCASIONS AND HOLIDAYS. I LIKE TO KEEP THE FILLING SIMPLE, BUT FEEL FREE TO EXPERIMENT WITH OTHER VEGETABLES, MEATS, AND EVEN PASTA SHAPES. HERE CHICKEN, TORTELLINI, AND PAPPARDELLE ARE LAYERED WITH CHEESE AND BÉCHAMEL SAUCE AND BAKED IN A FLAKY PIE CRUST.

FLAKY PASTRY

2 cups all-purpose flour

½ teaspoon salt

10 tablespoons cold unsalted butter, cut into ½-inch pieces

1 large egg yolk

¼ cup ice water

CHICKEN & PASTA FILLING

2 tablespoons olive oil

2 pounds chicken thighs, skinned

Salt & freshly ground pepper

2 medium-size carrots, finely chopped

1 small onion, finely chopped

1 large garlic clove, minced

1 teaspoon finely chopped fresh thyme

¼ teaspoon finely chopped fresh rosemary

¼ cup all-purpose flour

½ cup dry white wine

1 cup chicken broth, preferably homemade (p. 11)

3 tablespoons unsalted butter

2¾ cups milk

Prepare the flaky pastry: In a food processor, combine the flour and salt, pulsing to combine. Evenly distribute the pieces of butter on top of the flour and pulse until the mixture resembles coarse meal. In a small dish, beat the egg yolk with the ice water. With the machine running, pour in the egg mixture, pulsing just until the dough holds together. Divide the dough into thirds. Shape two pieces of dough into 6-inch discs. Roll the remaining dough into a 9-inch log. Wrap individually in plastic wrap and refrigerate for at least 1 hour or overnight.

On a lightly floured surface, roll each dough disc into a 10-inch round, about ⅛ inch thick. Trim each into a 9-inch circle. Transfer one of the circles to a baking sheet lined with waxed paper and refrigerate. Fit the second circle into the bottom of an 8-x-3-inch springform pan, pressing the dough into the bottom and just slightly up the sides. Cut the dough log lengthwise in half and roll out each half into a 3½-x-13-inch-long strip. (These strips will form the sides of the timballo.) Trim one long edge of

each dough strip and fit the strips snugly into the springform pan, over-lapping them slightly and allowing the top edge of the dough to extend over the top of the pan. Press the dough edges together to seal the seams. Trim the top edge of the dough to a ½-inch overhang. Cut out leaves or other small decorative shapes using the dough scraps. Refrigerate the crust and cutouts until ready to use.

Prepare the chicken and pasta filling: In a large skillet, heat the oil over medium-high heat. Lightly season the chicken on both sides with salt and pepper. Put into the skillet and cook, without turning, for 8 minutes, or until crusty and browned. Turn the chicken and reduce the heat to medium-low. Partially cover and cook for about 12 minutes, or until the chicken is cooked through. Transfer to a plate, cover loosely with foil, and set aside.

Pour off all but 1 tablespoon of the oil from the skillet. Place the skillet over medium heat, add the carrots, onion, garlic, thyme, and rosemary, and cook, stirring, for 4 minutes or until softened. Stir in 1 tablespoon of the flour and cook, stirring, for 30 seconds. Stir in the wine and cook until it has nearly evaporated, scraping to loosen any browned bits in the bottom of the pan. Add the broth, reduce the heat to medium-low, and cook, stirring, for 8 to 10 minutes, or until the sauce is reduced to about ⅔ cup. Pour the sauce through a fine-mesh strainer set over a medium-size bowl, pressing on the solids to extract as much liquid as possible. Set the sauce aside and reserve the vegetables. Remove the chicken from the bones and

8 ounces cheese-, wild
   mushroom-, or pumpkin-
   filled tortellini

8 ounces pappardelle

¾ cup freshly grated Parmesan
   cheese

1 large egg yolk beaten with
   1 tablespoon water, for
   egg wash

cut into ½-inch pieces. Transfer the chicken to a medium-size bowl, stir in the reserved vegetables, and set aside.

Melt the butter in a medium-size saucepan over medium-high heat. Add the remaining 3 tablespoons flour and cook, whisking, for about 1 minute. Add the milk, whisking, and bring to a boil. Reduce the heat to medium and cook, stirring occasionally, for 4 minutes, or until thickened. Stir in the reserved sauce, 1¼ teaspoons salt, and ¼ teaspoon pepper. Remove from the heat and set aside.

Cook the tortellini and pappardelle in separate pots following the basic method (page 13), until al dente. Drain well.

Preheat the oven to 425°F.

Remove the springform pan from the refrigerator. Spread half of the tortellini in a single layer over the bottom of the crust. Top with half of the chicken and half of the pappardelle. Cover with half of the sauce and sprinkle with half of the cheese. Repeat the layers with the remaining ingredients. Place the remaining dough round on top of the filling, pressing lightly to compact the ingredients. Brush the top of the dough with the egg wash. Bring the dough overhang up and over the top crust and press lightly to seal. Decorate the top dough seam with the dough cutouts, attaching them to the dough with a little cold water. Lightly brush the top of the timballo with egg wash and cut a vent hole in the center.

Bake the timballo on the center rack of the oven for 45 minutes, or until the top is deep golden. Cover loosely with foil, reduce the heat to 375°F, and bake for another 45 minutes. Let the timballo rest for 15 minutes.

Place the timballo on a large serving plate. Carefully remove the springform ring, cut into wedges, and serve.

WEIGHTS

Ounces and Pounds	Metric Equivalent
1/4 ounce	7 grams
1/3 ounce	10 g
1/2 ounce	14 g
1 ounce	28 g
1 1/2 ounces	42 g
1 3/4 ounces	50 g
2 ounces	57 g
3 ounces	85 g
3 1/2 ounces	100 g
4 ounces (1/4 pound)	114 g
6 ounces	170 g
8 ounces (1/2 pound)	227 g
9 ounces	250 g
16 ounces (1 pound)	464 g

TEMPERATURE

°F (*Fahrenheit*)	°C (*Centigrade or Celsius*)
32 (water freezes)	0
200	95
212 (water boils)	100
250	120
275	135
300 (slow oven)	150
325	160
350 (moderate oven)	175
375	190
400 (hot oven)	205
425	220
450 (very hot oven)	232
475	245
500 (extremely hot oven)	260

LIQUID MEASURES

tsp.: teaspoon / Tbs.: tablespoon

Spoons and Cups	Metric Equivalents
1/4 tsp.	1.23 milliliters
1/2 tsp.	2.5 ml
3/4 tsp.	3.7 ml
1 tsp.	5 ml
1 dessertspoon	10 ml
1 Tbs. (3 tsp.)	15 ml
2 Tbs. (1 ounce)	30 ml
1/4 cup	60 ml
1/3 cup	80 ml
1/2 cup	120 ml
2/3 cup	160 ml
3/4 cup	180 ml
1 cup (8 ounces)	240 ml
2 cups (1 pint)	480 ml
3 cups	720 ml
4 cups (1 quart)	1 liter
4 quarts (1 gallon)	3.75 liters

LENGTH

U.S. Measurements	Metric Equivalent
1/8 inch	3 mm
1/4 inch	6 mm
3/8 inch	1 cm
1/2 inch	1.2 cm
3/4 inch	2 cm
1 inch	2.5 cm
1 1/4 inches	3.1 cm
1 1/2 inches	3.7 cm
2 inches	5 cm
3 inches	7.5 cm
4 inches	10 cm
5 inches	12.5 cm

APPROXIMATE EQUIVALENTS

1 kilo is slightly more than 2 pounds
1 liter is slightly more than 1 quart
1 meter is slightly over 3 feet
1 centimeter is approximately 3/8 inch

WINTER PASTA

INDEX

Baked Rigatoni with Sun-Dried Tomatoes	49
Bucatini with Tuna Sauce	23
Chicken & Pasta Timballo	53
Chicken Broth	11
Escarole-Bean Soup with Tomato Oil	7
Fettuccine with Bacon & Brie	19
Fish Chowder with Capellini & Rouille	12
Fish Stock	13
Fusilli Marinara with Two Ricottas	24
Golden Orecchiette	15
Hearty Lamb Ragu	39
Macaroni ai Quattro Formaggi	43
Minestrone with Toasted Pastina	6
Mussel Chowder with Chorizo	14
Paella with Fideo	50
Pappardelle with Chicken Livers	26
Pappardelle with Wild Mushrooms	16
Pasta Lendiche	9
Pasta with Ragu Bolognese	30
Pastitsio	50
Rich Chicken Broth	11
Rigatoni with Fennel & Tomatoes	29
Rigatoni with Tomato Meat Sauce	31
Savory Pappardelle with Rabbit	36
Seafood & Saffron Risotto	34
Spaghetti alla Arrabbiata	27
Spaghetti alla Carbonara	18
Tortellini with Crisp Sage	21
Veal & Porcini Mushroom Ragu	40
Vermicelli with Broccoli Rabe	22
Wild Mushroom & Leek Timbale	44
Winter Lasagne	47
Winter Vegetable Soup with Pesto	10

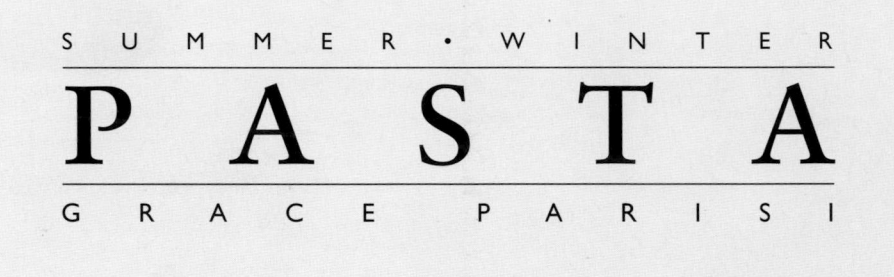

SUMMER · WINTER

PASTA

GRACE PARISI

Photography by

MELANIE ACEVEDO

QUILL

WILLIAM MORROW AND COMPANY

NEW YORK

It is the policy of William Morrow and Company, Inc., and its imprints and affiliates,
recognizing the importance of preserving what has been written, to
print the books we publish on acid-free paper, and we exert our best efforts to that end.

Library of Congress Cataloging-in-Publication Data

Parisi, Grace.
Summer / winter pasta / Grace Parisi.
p.   cm.
ISBN 0-688-15213-9
1. Cookery (Pasta)   1. Title.
TX809 .M17P34   1997
641.8'22—dc21
97-6248
CIP

ISBN: 0-688-15213-9

Editor: DEBORAH MINTCHEFF
Designer: SUSI OBERHELMAN
Assistant Editor: SARAH STEWART
Assistant Designer: AYAKO HOSONO
Food Stylist: KEVIN CRAFTS
Prop Stylist: ROBYN GLASER

First Edition

1 2 3 4 5 6 7 8 9 10

PRODUCED BY SMALLWOOD & STEWART, INC., NEW YORK CITY

PRINTED IN SINGAPORE

CONTENTS

SUMMER PASTA

introduction 4

SUMMER SAUCES 6

SALADS 17

LIGHT MEALS 29

SAVORY SUPPERS 43

conversion chart 53

index 54

PASTA

SUMMER

INTRODUCTION

For me, summer meals should be uncomplicated and full of fresh flavors; I want my food to be simple and easy to prepare, in keeping with the season. Now is the time for salads and sandwiches, grills and picnics. And now is the time to use locally grown produce at its peak, the way our mothers and grandmothers did before supermarkets and air transportation. At farm stands and in farmers markets, I look for heirloom tomatoes; sweet succulent corn; aromatic garden-fresh herbs; bell peppers and chiles; tender summer squash; and green and yellow beans of every variety.

I've incorporated both these ideas in the recipes that follow. They're all easy-to-prepare dishes that let the flavors of the ingredients shine through—a summer arrabbiata in an uncooked sauce of ripe tomatoes and fresh chiles, a lemon-spiked salad with roasted peppers and asparagus, a couscous with fresh vegetable ratatouille. I hope they'll become memorable summer meals for you and your family.

CHANGING SEASONS: HOW TO USE THIS BOOK

When you feel like moving on to winter dishes, just flip the book over and you'll find a whole new set of recipes for cold-weather comfort waiting for you. Each half is a mini book unto itself, complete with its own page numbers and index.

S U M M E R
P A S T A

PASTA WITH OVEN-DRIED TOMATO TAPENADE

Serves 4 to 6

OVEN-DRIED TOMATOES

2 pounds plum tomatoes

1 small head garlic, cloves
separated but not peeled

About ½ cup extra-virgin
olive oil

TOMATO TAPENADE

2 tablespoons chopped fresh
flat-leaf parsley

2 anchovy fillets, minced

1 tablespoon red wine vinegar

Salt & freshly ground pepper

1 pound penne rigate, gemelli,
or pennette

Freshly grated Parmesan cheese,
for serving

THE QUALITY OF THE DRIED TOMATOES YOU
FIND IN GOURMET STORES IS NO MATCH FOR THESE, WHICH
ARE THE BASIS OF A RICH SAUCE.

Preheat the oven to 275°F. Oil a large shallow nonstick baking pan.

Prepare the oven-dried tomatoes: Bring a large saucepan of water to a boil over high heat. Cut a small X in the bottom of each tomato. Put the tomatoes into the boiling water for 30 seconds; transfer to a large bowl of ice water for 1 minute. Drain, slip the skins off the tomatoes, then halve and seed. Place the tomatoes, cut side down, in the baking pan and scatter the garlic cloves over. Roast for 1 hour, or until the tomatoes begin to look dry. Turn the tomatoes over and roast for another hour. Turn off the oven, prop the door open slightly with the handle of a wooden spoon, and let the tomatoes continue to dry in the oven for 1 hour.

Peel the garlic and arrange in alternating layers with the tomatoes in a large canning jar. Pour enough oil over to cover completely. Tightly cover the jar and store in the refrigerator for up to 2 months.

Prepare the tomato tapenade: Drain the tomatoes and garlic, reserving the oil. Finely chop the tomatoes and transfer to a large serving bowl with the parsley, anchovies, vinegar, and 3 tablespoons of the reserved oil. Season with salt and pepper and set aside.

Cook the pasta following the basic method (page 9), until al dente. Toss the pasta with the tapenade. Serve immediately, passing the Parmesan on the side. (Refrigerate the remaining tomato oil for another use.)

LINGUINE WITH SMOKY TOMATO COULIS

Serves 4

6 large garlic cloves, unpeeled

2 pounds plum tomatoes, quartered & seeded

1 small fresh rosemary sprig

¼ cup extra-virgin olive oil

Salt & freshly ground pepper

1 tablespoon balsamic vinegar

12 ounces linguine, spaghetti, or long fusilli

Asiago cheese shavings (removed with a vegetable peeler), for garnish

THE RIDGED CAST-IRON PAN USED IN THIS RECIPE GIVES THE TOMATOES A SMOKY FLAVOR WITHOUT HAVING TO LIGHT A FIRE. IF YOU PREFER, SET THE TOMATOES ON AN OILED VEGETABLE GRILL RACK, AND GRILL OVER A MEDIUM-HOT FIRE.

Place a cast-iron grill pan over medium heat. Add the garlic cloves and cook, turning frequently, for 15 minutes, or until soft and blackened in spots. Transfer to a small dish and cool, then remove the skins. Set aside.

Put the tomatoes and rosemary into a large bowl. Drizzle with 1 tablespoon of the oil and season with salt and pepper, tossing. Place the rosemary sprig and tomatoes, skin side down, in the grill pan. Cook, turning often, for 7 minutes, or until the tomatoes are soft and the skin is blackened. Transfer to a large bowl, cover, and let sit for 10 minutes.

Remove the rosemary leaves from the sprig. In a blender, combine the tomatoes, garlic, rosemary, and vinegar, pulsing until smooth. With the machine running, add the remaining 3 tablespoons oil in a slow steady stream and blend until thick and smooth. Press the sauce through a fine-mesh strainer set over a medium-size bowl, pressing on the solids with the back of a spoon. Season with salt and pepper and cover to keep warm.

Meanwhile, cook the pasta following the basic method (page 9), until al dente. Drain well and transfer to a large serving bowl. Add the tomato coulis, toss well, and sprinkle with the Asiago shavings.

FUSILLI CON SUGO FRANCESCA

Serves 4

JUICY, RIPE TOMATOES ARE COMBINED
WITH SWEET RICOTTA CHEESE, LEMON ZEST, FRESH
FLAT-LEAF PARSLEY, AND CHIVES TO
MAKE THIS FRESH-TASTING, CREAMY SAUCE. FOR
THE BEST FLAVOR, USE FRESH
RICOTTA CHEESE PURCHASED IN A CHEESE SHOP.

1 pound tomatoes, coarsely chopped

1 cup ricotta cheese, pressed through a strainer

1 tablespoon finely chopped fresh flat-leaf parsley

1 tablespoon finely chopped fresh chives

¾ teaspoon grated lemon zest

Salt & freshly ground pepper

12 ounces long fusilli

In a large serving bowl, combine the tomatoes, ricotta, parsley, chives, and lemon zest. Season with salt and pepper and set aside.

Cook the pasta following the basic method, until al dente. Drain well, reserving ¼ cup of the pasta water. Toss the pasta with the tomato ricotta sauce, adding some of the reserved pasta water, 1 tablespoon at a time, if the mixture seems dry. Season with salt and pepper, if desired, toss, and serve immediately in large shallow bowls.

BASIC PASTA COOKING METHOD

In a large pot, bring 4 quarts of cold water to a boil over high heat; add 2 tablespoons salt. Add the pasta and cook, stirring occasionally to prevent the pasta from sticking, until al dente. (Use the cooking time indicated on the pasta box as a guide since it varies, depending on the brand and type of pasta.) To test for doneness, cut through a piece of pasta. When the pasta is al dente, it is considered firm to the bite—it should not be hard. Drain the pasta by pouring it into a colander; shake out the excess water. The pasta should not be rinsed unless specified in the recipe.

PENNE WITH SUMMER ARRABBIATA

2 large beefsteak or heirloom
    tomatoes

3 ounces thinly sliced prosciutto,
    cut crosswise into ¼-inch-
    wide strips

1 large garlic clove, minced

1 small red chile, such as Thai or
    serrano, seeded & minced

2 tablespoons fruity extra-virgin
    olive oil

Salt

12 ounces penne rigate, gemelli,
    or pennette

Parmesan or Grano Padano cheese
    shavings (removed with a
    vegetable peeler), for garnish

THIS RECIPE TAKES FULL ADVANTAGE OF SUMMER'S
BOUNTY OF BEAUTIFUL HEIRLOOM TOMATOES AND, AT THE
SAME TIME, PAYS HOMAGE TO THE TRADITIONAL
SPICY TOMATO ARRABBIATA SAUCE. HERE, FRESH CHILE
AND PROSCIUTTO STAND IN FOR THE MORE COMMONLY USED
CRUSHED RED PEPPER FLAKES AND PANCETTA.

Bring a large saucepan of water to a boil over high heat. Use a paring knife to cut a small X in the bottom of each tomato. Put the tomatoes into the boiling water for 30 seconds. Use a slotted spoon to transfer the tomatoes to a large bowl of ice water; let sit for about 1 minute. Drain, then slip the skins off the tomatoes, and cut crosswise in half.

Working over a strainer set over a large bowl, squeeze the tomatoes to remove the juice and seeds. Discard the seeds. Coarsely chop the tomatoes and add them to the strained juice along with the prosciutto, garlic, chile, and oil. Season with salt, stir, and set aside.

Cook the pasta following the basic method (page 9), until al dente. Drain well. Combine the pasta with the tomato mixture, tossing until well mixed. Divide among large shallow soup bowls, sprinkle with the Parmesan shavings, and serve.

LINGUINE WITH LEMON WALNUT PESTO

Serves 4 to 6

TOASTED WALNUTS GROUND WITH LEMON
ZEST AND FRUITY OLIVE OIL AND SERVED WITH LINGUINE
MAKES A TASTY MEDITERRANEAN VARIATION
ON THE MORE USUAL ASIAN COLD NOODLES WITH
PEANUT SAUCE. ALMONDS AND PECANS
BOTH WORK NICELY IN PLACE OF THE WALNUTS.

LEMON WALNUT PESTO

1 cup walnuts, toasted

1 tablespoon minced lemon zest

¼ teaspoon crushed red pepper
    flakes

¼ cup fruity extra-virgin olive oil

1½ teaspoons fresh lemon juice

Salt

1 pound linguine

1 tablespoon shredded fresh lemon
    balm*, for garnish (optional)

In a food processor, combine the walnuts, lemon zest, and red pepper flakes, pulsing until finely chopped. With the machine running, add the oil in a slow steady stream, pulsing until a coarse paste forms. Transfer to a large bowl, stir in the lemon juice, and season with salt. Set aside.

Cook the pasta following the basic method (page 9), until al dente. Drain well, reserving ¼ cup of the pasta water. Add the pasta to the pesto and toss, adding some of the reserved pasta water, 1 tablespoon at a time, if the pasta seems dry. Toss until mixed well.

To serve, divide the pasta among large bowls and sprinkle with the lemon balm, if desired.

*Lemon balm is a member of the mint family and has a lemon-mint fragrance. It can be easily grown from seed and plants can be purchased at nurseries and farmers markets. Lemon thyme is a good substitute when lemon balm is not available.

Serves 4

SWEET TOASTED ALMONDS AND FRAGRANT
ANISE SEEDS ADD DEPTH TO THIS VARIATION ON THE
CLASSIC PASTA WITH GARLIC AND OIL.

12 ounces thin spaghetti

¼ cup extra-virgin olive oil

⅓ cup sliced unblanched almonds

3 garlic cloves, thinly sliced

1 teaspoon anise seeds

2 tablespoons chopped fresh
   flat-leaf parsley

Salt & freshly ground pepper

Cook the pasta following the basic method (page 9), until al dente. Drain well. Transfer to a large serving bowl and cover to keep warm.

Meanwhile, in a small skillet, heat the oil over medium-high heat. Add the almonds and garlic and cook, stirring, for 2 minutes, or until golden brown. Add the anise seeds and cook, stirring, for about 30 seconds, or until fragrant.

Pour the sauce over the pasta, sprinkle with the parsley, and season with salt and pepper. Toss until well mixed and serve immediately.

LINGUINE & PESTO GENOVESE

Serves 4 to 6

PESTO GENOVESE

1½ cups packed fresh basil leaves

2 tablespoons packed fresh
      flat-leaf parsley leaves

2 garlic cloves

½ cup extra-virgin olive oil

¼ cup plus 2 tablespoons freshly
      grated Pecorino Romano
      cheese, plus additional,
      for serving

¼ cup pine nuts, toasted

1 tablespoon unsalted butter,
      at room temperature

Salt & freshly ground pepper

1 pound linguine, penne rigate,
      or spaghetti

TRADITIONALLY, THIS MUCH LOVED BASIL SAUCE IS POUNDED TO A PASTE IN A MORTAR WITH A PESTLE, WHICH GIVES THE PESTO A SLIGHTLY COARSER TEXTURE THAN WHEN IT IS PREPARED IN A FOOD PROCESSOR. PESTO IS ONE OF THE EASIEST AND MOST SATISFYING WAYS TO PRESERVE A BOUNTIFUL CROP OF BASIL, SINCE IT REFRIGERATES WELL. IF YOU PLAN TO FREEZE A BATCH OF PESTO, LEAVE OUT THE PINE NUTS AND PARMESAN CHEESE. ADD THEM WHEN YOU ARE READY TO USE THE SAUCE.

Prepare the pesto Genovese: In a food processor or blender, combine the basil, parsley, and garlic, pulsing until finely chopped. With the machine running, pour in the oil in a slow steady stream, processing until very smooth. Add the Romano, pine nuts, and butter and process, pulsing, until the nuts are finely chopped. Transfer to a large bowl and season with salt and pepper.

Cook the pasta following the basic method (page 9), until al dente. Drain the pasta, reserving ¼ cup of the pasta water. Toss the pasta with the pesto, adding some of the reserved pasta water, 1 tablespoon at a time, if the mixture seems dry. Toss until mixed well.

To serve, divide the pasta among large bowls and pass additional Romano cheese alongside.

SPAGHETTI WITH SALSINA VERDE

Serves 4 to 6

ANCHOVIES AND CAPERS ADD AN UNEXPECTED
PUNCH TO THIS HERBAL PESTO. SINCE
IT IS A BIT MORE ASSERTIVE THAN CLASSIC PESTO
GENOVESE, IT IS BEST WHEN SERVED WITH
THIN STRANDS OF PASTA RATHER THAN A SHAPE
WITH LOTS OF NOOKS AND CRANNIES.

SALSINA VERDE

¼ cup plus 2 tablespoons
   extra-virgin olive oil

4 anchovy fillets

2 large garlic cloves, minced

1 cup tightly packed fresh flat-leaf
   parsley leaves

¼ cup capers, rinsed

1 tablespoon fresh oregano leaves

1 teaspoon fresh thyme leaves

1½ teaspoons white wine vinegar

Salt & freshly ground pepper

1 pound spaghetti, thin spaghetti,
   or bucatini

Freshly grated Pecorino Romano
   cheese, for serving

Prepare the salsina verde: In a small skillet, combine the oil, anchovies, and garlic over medium heat. Cook, stirring, for 1 minute, or until the garlic is golden. Transfer to a small bowl and cool.

In a food processor or blender, combine the parsley, capers, oregano, thyme, and vinegar, pulsing until the herbs are finely chopped. Add the garlic oil mixture and process until smooth. Transfer to a large bowl and season with salt and pepper.

Meanwhile, cook the pasta following the basic method (page 9), until al dente. Drain well, reserving ¼ cup of the pasta water. Toss the sauce with the pasta, adding some of the reserved pasta water, 1 tablespoon at a time, if the mixture seems dry. Serve immediately in large bowls, passing the Romano separately.

PASTA WITH OLIVE-CAPER PESTO

Serves   4

OLIVE-CAPER PESTO

2 tablespoons fresh mint leaves

2 tablespoons capers, rinsed

1 large garlic clove, chopped

½ teaspoon grated lemon zest

⅛ teaspoon crushed red
    pepper flakes

3 tablespoons extra-virgin olive oil

½ pound assorted olives
    (about 1 cup), pitted

Salt & freshly ground pepper

1 pound spaghetti, gemelli,
    or pennette

¼ cup freshly grated Parmesan
    cheese

FOR AN INTERESTING MIX OF FLAVORS
AND TEXTURES IN THIS PESTO, USE A COMBINATION
OF BOTH BRINE- AND OIL-CURED OLIVES.
LIGHTLY CURED GREEN SICILIAN, EARTHY OIL-
CURED MOROCCAN, TANGY NIÇOISE, AND KALAMATA
OLIVES GO TOGETHER NICELY.

Prepare the olive-caper pesto: In a food processor, combine the mint, capers, garlic, lemon zest, red pepper flakes, and oil. Process, pulsing, until finely chopped, scraping down the sides of the bowl once or twice. Add the olives and pulse to a chunky puree, leaving some of the olives coarsely chopped. Transfer to a large serving bowl and season with salt and pepper.

Cook the pasta following the basic method (page 9), until al dente. Drain well, reserving ¼ cup of the pasta water.

Toss the pasta with the olive pesto, adding some of the reserved pasta water, 1 tablespoon at a time, if the mixture seems dry. Sprinkle with the Parmesan, transfer to large shallow bowls, and serve.

TOMATO-MOZZARELLA SALAD WITH PASTA

Serves 4 to 6

THE FLAVORFUL JUICES OF TOMATOES ARE
BLENDED WITH HERB-INFUSED OIL TO MAKE A DELICATE
DRESSING FOR THIS VARIATION ON THE
CLASSIC TOMATO, MOZZARELLA, AND BASIL SALAD.
I'VE USED ROUGHLY BROKEN PAPPARDELLE
HERE, BUT YOU CAN USE PENNE, ROTINI, GEMELLI,
OR FARFALLE IF YOU PREFER.

1 cup tightly packed fresh basil leaves, plus 2 tablespoons shredded basil, for garnish

½ cup packed fresh flat-leaf parsley leaves

3 tablespoons snipped fresh chives

1 large garlic clove

3 tablespoons extra-virgin olive oil

3 tablespoons vegetable oil

2 large tomatoes, chopped

Salt & freshly ground pepper

8 ounces pappardelle, broken into 1-inch lengths

8 ounces salted fresh mozzarella cheese, cut into ¾-inch cubes

Bring a small saucepan of water to a boil over high heat. Add the whole basil leaves and blanch for 10 seconds, or just until wilted and bright green. Transfer to a strainer and rinse under cold running water until cool. Using your hands, squeeze out the excess water.

In a food processor or blender, combine the basil, parsley, chives, garlic, olive oil, and vegetable oil, processing until very smooth. Transfer to a large bowl, add the tomatoes, season with salt and pepper, and toss.

Cook the pasta following the basic method (page 9), until al dente. Drain, then rinse under cold running water until cool; drain well. Pat the pasta dry with paper towels. Add the pasta and mozzarella to the tomatoes, season with salt and pepper, and toss. Let sit for 15 minutes to allow the flavors to blend.

Transfer the pasta to large serving bowls, garnish with the shredded basil, and serve.

ORECCHIETTE GIARDINERE

Serves 4 to 6

½ pound fresh fava beans, shelled

¼ pound asparagus, tough ends removed & cut into 1½-inch pieces

¼ pound yellow wax beans, trimmed & cut into 1½-inch pieces

1 medium-size carrot, thinly sliced

1 yellow bell pepper, halved, cored, seeded & thinly sliced

1 small zucchini, halved lengthwise & cut crosswise into thin slices

1 red chile, such as Thai or serrano, thinly sliced, or ¼ teaspoon crushed red pepper flakes

1 tablespoon sugar

¼ teaspoon fennel seeds

Salt

¼ cup white wine vinegar

2 tablespoons cold water

½ cup Niçoise olives, pitted

¼ cup extra-virgin olive oil

4 ounces orecchiette

4 ounces marinated bocconcini (very small mozzarella balls), halved, if desired

Freshly ground pepper

CRISP AND COLORFUL SUMMER VEGETABLES ARE LIGHTLY PICKLED IN A SWEET AND TANGY MARINADE. COMBINED WITH ORECCHIETTE AND CREAMY FRESH MOZZARELLA, THEY MAKE A TASTY SUMMERTIME MIDDAY MEAL.

Bring a large pot of water to a boil over high heat. Blanch the fava beans for 3 minutes. Remove with a slotted spoon to a colander and cool under cold running water. Slip the skins off the fava beans, transfer to a large bowl, and set aside.

Bring the water back to a boil and add salt. Blanch the asparagus, wax beans, carrot, and bell pepper together for 3 minutes, or until crisp-tender. Drain and cool with the fava beans. Blanch the zucchini for 30 seconds and combine with the other vegetables.

In a small saucepan, combine the chile, sugar, fennel seeds, 1 teaspoon salt, vinegar, and water. Cook over medium heat, stirring, until the sugar has dissolved. Pour over the vegetables. Cover and refrigerate, stirring occasionally, for about 1 hour, or until chilled. Add the olives and oil to the vegetables and toss thoroughly. Let marinate in the refrigerator for at least 1 or up to 8 hours.

Cook the pasta following the basic method (page 9), until al dente. Drain and transfer to a large serving bowl. Add the vegetables and bocconcini and toss until mixed. Season with salt and pepper, toss, and serve.

PANZANELLA WITH PENNETTE

Serves 4

THE SMOKED CHICKEN MAKES THIS A
MORE SUBSTANTIAL, FLAVORFUL VERSION OF THE CLASSIC
PANZANELLA SALAD. IT'S BEST TO SERVE THIS
SALAD RIGHT AWAY SO THE BREAD STAYS CRISP, ALTHOUGH
IT'S STILL DELICIOUS WHEN A BIT SOGGY.

8 ounces pennette

½ (1-pound) loaf Tuscan bread,
cut into 1-inch cubes

¼ cup plus 3 tablespoons
extra-virgin olive oil

1 large tomato, cut into ¾-inch
chunks

⅓ cup thinly sliced red onion

¼ cup loosely packed torn fresh
basil leaves

¼ cup loosely packed torn fresh
flat-leaf parsley leaves

1 smoked chicken breast (½ pound),
skinned & shredded (optional)

3 tablespoons red wine vinegar

Salt & freshly ground pepper

Preheat the oven to 350°F.

Cook the pennette following the basic method (page 9), until al dente. Drain well, then rinse briefly under cold running water, and drain thoroughly. Set aside.

On a large baking sheet, toss the bread cubes with 1 tablespoon of the oil and spread out in a single layer. Toast the bread cubes in the oven, turning once or twice, for about 6 minutes, or until crisp and golden.

In a large serving bowl, combine the pasta, bread cubes, tomato, onion, basil, parsley, and chicken, if using.

Whisk the vinegar with the remaining ¼ cup plus 2 tablespoons oil in a small bowl. Drizzle over the salad and toss until well coated. Season with salt and pepper, toss again, and serve immediately.

ORZO SALAD WITH PEPPERS & ASPARAGUS

Serves 4 to 6

3 large red, yellow, or orange
    bell peppers

1 tablespoon fresh lemon juice

3 tablespoons extra-virgin olive oil

Salt & freshly ground pepper

1 pound thin asparagus, tough
    ends removed & cut into
    1½-inch pieces

1¼ cups orzo

¼ cup chopped fresh flat-leaf
    parsley

1 teaspoon finely shredded
    lemon zest

SMOKY ROASTED PEPPERS ARE COMBINED WITH ASPARAGUS, LEMONY ROASTED PEPPER DRESSING, AND TINY RICE-SHAPED PASTA IN THIS SIMPLE SUMMERY SALAD. SERVE WARM OR SLIGHTLY CHILLED, NOT COLD.

Roast the peppers over a gas or charcoal flame, or under a broiler, turning occasionally, for about 15 minutes, or until blackened on all sides. Transfer to a large plastic bag, seal tightly, and let steam for 10 minutes. When cool enough to handle, peel, core, and seed the peppers.

Cut 2 of the bell peppers into ¼-inch-wide strips. Set aside. Cut the remaining bell pepper into coarse chunks, put into a blender along with the lemon juice, and blend until pureed. With the machine running, add the oil in a slow steady stream, blending until thick and smooth. Transfer to a small bowl, season with salt and pepper, and set aside.

Bring a medium-size saucepan of salted water to a boil over high heat. Add the asparagus and cook for 3 minutes, or until crisp-tender. Drain, rinse under cold running water until cool, and drain well. Set aside.

Cook the orzo following the basic method (page 9), until al dente. Drain, rinse under cold running water until cool, and drain thoroughly. Transfer to a large serving bowl and add the bell pepper strips, asparagus, parsley, lemon zest, and bell pepper sauce. Season with salt and pepper and toss until mixed well. Serve.

FARFALLINI & CHICKEN WITH CHIVE DRESSING

Serves 4

THIS DISH COMBINES THE BASIC INGREDIENTS OF TWO FAVORITE SALADS: CHICKEN AND PASTA. LITTLE BOW TIES ARE COMBINED WITH SAUTEED CHICKEN, SNOW PEAS, CORN, AND CRISPY PANCETTA, CREATING A SALAD WHOSE TEXTURE AND FLAVOR WILL SATISFY ANY FOOD CRAVINGS.

1 cup farfallini

2 boneless skinless chicken breast halves (about 10 ounces)

Salt & freshly ground pepper

2 ounces thinly sliced pancetta, coarsely chopped

2 ears fresh corn, kernels cut off

¼ pound snow peas, strings removed & cut diagonally into julienne

3 tablespoons mayonnaise

2 tablespoons minced fresh chives, plus additional, for garnish

1½ tablespoons sherry vinegar

2 tablespoons olive oil

Cook the farfallini following the basic method (page 9), until al dente. Drain, cool under cold running water, and drain again. Transfer to a large bowl, cover, and set aside.

Put the chicken between pieces of plastic wrap and pound to ¼-inch thickness. Season the chicken with salt and pepper and set aside.

In a large skillet, cook the pancetta over medium-high heat, for about 4 minutes, or until browned. Using a slotted spoon, transfer to a paper towel–lined bowl. Add the chicken to the skillet and cook for 2 minutes on each side, or until cooked through. Transfer to a cutting board and cool. Cut the chicken across the grain into thin strips. Add to the pasta along with any accumulated juices.

Return the skillet to medium-high heat. Add the corn and snow peas and cook, stirring, for 1 minute, or until barely tender. Add the corn and snow peas to the pasta and set aside until cool.

In a food processor, combine the mayonnaise, chives, and vinegar, blending until smooth. With the machine running, add the oil in a slow stream, blending until smooth. Pour over the pasta, season with salt and pepper, and toss. Transfer to a serving bowl and garnish with the chives.

GRILLED SEAFOOD
PASTA SALAD

½ pound medium-size shrimp,
    peeled & deveined

½ pound large sea scallops

2 large garlic cloves, minced

1 teaspoon grated lemon zest

2 tablespoons olive oil

Freshly ground pepper

8 ounces small shell-shaped pasta

1 large red bell pepper

Salt

¼ pound snow peas, strings
    removed & cut crosswise
    into 1-inch pieces

LEMON MAYONNAISE

¼ cup mayonnaise

¼ cup sour cream

1½ tablespoons fresh lemon juice

1 teaspoon chopped fresh tarragon

1 head Bibb lettuce, leaves
    separated & washed

THIS ELEGANT SEAFOOD SALAD IS PERFECTLY SUITED
FOR A FIRST COURSE, SERVED SLIGHTLY CHILLED WITH A
DRY CHAMPAGNE AND FRENCH BREAD CROUTES.

In a large bowl, combine the shrimp, scallops, garlic, lemon zest, and oil. Season generously with pepper. Cover with plastic wrap and marinate in the refrigerator for at least 2 or up to 4 hours.

Preheat a grill to medium and brush with oil, or place a stovetop grill pan over medium-high heat.

Cook the pasta following the basic method (page 9), until al dente. Drain, rinse under cold water, and drain. Transfer to a bowl; set aside.

Grill the bell pepper, turning occasionally, for about 15 minutes, or until the skin is blackened on all sides. Put the pepper into a plastic bag, seal tightly, and let steam for 10 minutes. When cool enough to handle, peel, core, seed, and finely chop the pepper. Set aside.

Season the shrimp and scallops with salt. Grill, turning once, for 4 minutes, or until cooked through. Cut into ½-inch pieces. Set aside.

Bring a small saucepan of salted water to a boil over high heat. Cook the snow peas for 2 minutes, or until crisp-tender. Drain and rinse until cool. Add the snow peas, bell pepper, shrimp, and scallops to the pasta.

Prepare the lemon mayonnaise: Whisk together all the lemon mayonnaise ingredients in a small bowl. Season with salt and pepper, add to the pasta salad, and toss until mixed well.

Arrange the lettuce on plates, top with the pasta salad, and serve.

GRILLED SALMON
& PASTA SALAD

Serves 4

8 ounces farfalle

1 pound skinless salmon fillet

Salt & freshly ground pepper

LEMON-HERB MAYONNAISE

¼ cup mayonnaise

2 tablespoons finely chopped
fresh flat-leaf parsley

2 large scallions, cut into
1-inch pieces

½ teaspoon grated lemon zest

3 tablespoons fresh lemon juice

¼ cup light olive oil

Salt & freshly ground pepper

¼ pound sugar snap peas,
strings removed

1 English cucumber, peeled, halved
lengthwise & thinly sliced
crosswise

2 small bunches watercress, tough
stems removed & washed

THIS VERSATILE SALAD IS EQUALLY WELL SUITED FOR A FAMILY PICNIC OR AN ELEGANT LUNCHEON. FOR A MORE CASUAL PRESENTATION, CHOP THE WATERCRESS AND TOSS IT WITH THE OTHER INGREDIENTS, RATHER THAN USING IT AS A BED FOR THE SALAD.

Preheat a grill to hot and brush with oil.

Cook the farfalle following the basic method (page 9), until al dente. Drain and rinse under cold running water until cool. Drain, transfer the pasta to a large bowl and cover. Set aside. Season the salmon with salt and pepper. Grill for about 6 minutes, turning once, or until charred and almost cooked through.

Prepare the lemon-herb mayonnaise: In a blender, combine the mayonnaise, parsley, scallions, lemon zest, and lemon juice, blending until the scallions are finely chopped. With the machine running, add the oil in a slow stream, blending until thick and smooth. Transfer to a small bowl and season with salt and pepper. Cover and refrigerate until ready to use.

Bring a small saucepan of water to a boil. Cook the sugar snap peas for 2 minutes, or until crisp-tender. Drain, rinse, and set aside.

Flake the salmon into large pieces. Add to the pasta along with any accumulated juices, the sugar snap peas, cucumber, and lemon-herb mayonnaise, and toss gently. Season with salt and pepper and toss again.

To serve, divide the watercress among serving plates and mound the pasta salad on top.

LOBSTER & FRESH CORN SALAD

Serves 4 to 6

LOBSTER AND CORN IS A CLASSIC SUMMER
COMBINATION, REMINISCENT OF SEASIDE CLAM BAKES.

8 ounces small shell-shaped pasta

2 live lobsters (1 to 1¼ pounds each)

2 ears fresh corn

¼ pound green or yellow wax beans, trimmed

BASIL MAYONNAISE

1 large egg

3 tablespoons pesto (homemade p. 14 or store-bought)

3 tablespoons fresh lemon juice

1 teaspoon Dijon mustard

1 garlic clove, minced

Pinch of sugar

1 cup olive oil

Salt & freshly ground pepper

½ red bell pepper, cored, seeded & cut into ⅛-inch-wide strips

Salt & freshly ground pepper

Lemon wedges & 2 tablespoons shredded fresh basil, for garnish

Cook the pasta following the basic method (page 9), until al dente. Drain, rinse under cold running water, and drain well. Set aside in a large bowl.

Bring a large pot of water to a rolling boil over high heat. Plunge the lobsters head first into the water and cook for 13 minutes. Remove the lobsters and cool under cold running water; drain. Twist off and remove the claws and tails. Use a knife to cut through the cartilage on the underside of each tail. Remove the tail meat and cut into ¼-inch-thick medallions. Crack the claws and remove the meat. Set aside in the refrigerator.

Bring a large saucepan of water to a boil over high heat. Cook the corn and beans for 3 minutes, or just until tender. Drain then rinse under cold running water. Using a sharp knife, cut the corn kernels from the cobs and the beans into 1½-inch pieces. Set aside.

Prepare the basil mayonnaise: In a blender, combine the egg, pesto, lemon juice, mustard, garlic, and sugar, blending until smooth. With the machine running, add the oil in a slow stream, blending until thick. Transfer to a small bowl and season with salt and pepper.

Add the lobster, corn, beans, bell pepper, and half of the basil mayonnaise to the pasta, tossing to combine. Season with salt and pepper and toss again. Transfer to a large serving bowl and garnish with the lemon wedges and basil. Pass the remaining basil mayonnaise separately.

LAMB & ACINI DI PEPE TABBOULEH

Serves 4

SPICED OIL

1 tablespoon vegetable oil

½ teaspoon ground cumin

¼ teaspoon ground cinnamon

⅛ teaspoon each ground allspice & red pepper

½ pound boneless loin of lamb, cut into ½-inch-thick medallions

1 cup acini di pepe

⅓ cup each loosely packed fresh mint & flat-leaf parsley leaves

¼ cup olive oil

1 large beefsteak or heirloom tomato, halved, seeded & cut into ¼-inch dice

3 kirby cucumbers, peeled & cut into ¼-inch dice

½ small red onion, cut into ¼-inch dice

1 teaspoon grated lemon zest

Salt & freshly ground pepper

2 to 3 tablespoons fresh lemon juice

1 large bunch arugula, trimmed & washed

Lemon wedges, for garnish

> ACINI DI PEPE, A TINY PASTA WHOSE NAME TRANSLATES AS PEPPERCORNS, WORKS WELL IN PLACE OF THE TRADITIONAL BULGAR IN TABBOULEH, THE TRADITIONAL MIDDLE EASTERN GRAIN DISH.

Prepare the spiced oil: Whisk together all the ingredients in a medium-size bowl. Add the lamb and toss to coat. Cover and refrigerate for 30 minutes.

Meanwhile, cook the pasta following the basic method (page 9), until al dente. Drain, rinse under cold water, and drain. Put into a bowl.

Preheat a grill to hot and brush with oil.

In a blender, combine the mint and parsley, pulsing until finely chopped. Remove half the chopped herbs to a small bowl; set aside. With the blender running, add the oil in a slow stream, blending until smooth.

Add the tomato, cucumbers, onion, lemon zest, mint-parsley oil, and the reserved chopped herbs to the pasta. Season with salt and pepper and add lemon juice to taste; toss. Set aside.

Season the lamb with salt. Grill for about 1½ minutes on each side for medium, or to the desired degree of doneness. Transfer to a cutting board, cover loosely with foil, and let rest for about 3 minutes. Using a sharp knife, cut the lamb into ¼-inch-thick strips and add, along with any accumulated juices, to the tabbouleh, tossing until mixed well.

Divide the arugula among serving plates, top with the tabbouleh, and garnish with the lemon wedges.

GREEK SALAD WITH PASTA & MINT

Serves 4

KALAMATA OLIVES, ANCHOVIES, AND FETA
CHEESE, THREE VERY ASSERTIVE COMPONENTS OF THE
CLASSIC GREEK SALAD, ARE TEAMED UP HERE
WITH PASTA AND A FRESH TASTING MINT-OREGANO
DRESSING. BLANCHING THE MINT LEAVES
KEEPS THE DRESSING A BEAUTIFUL BRIGHT GREEN.

1 cup tightly packed fresh mint
leaves, plus 2 tablespoons
shredded mint

1 tablespoon fresh oregano leaves

Salt

⅓ cup plus 1 tablespoon
extra-virgin olive oil

12 ounces medium-size
shell-shaped pasta

1 large tomato, coarsely chopped

20 Kalamata olives, halved & pitted

Freshly ground pepper

½ Vidalia onion, thinly sliced

½ red bell pepper, cored, seeded
& thinly sliced

4 anchovy fillets, chopped

1 cucumber, peeled, seeded
& cut into ½-inch dice

2 tablespoons fresh lemon juice

4 ounces feta cheese, crumbled
(about 1 cup)

Bring a small saucepan of water to a boil over high heat. Add the whole mint leaves and blanch for 10 seconds, or until wilted and bright green. Transfer to a strainer, rinse under cold running water until cool, and squeeze out the excess water.

In a blender, combine the blanched mint, oregano, ¼ teaspoon salt, and ⅓ cup of the oil, processing until smooth. Transfer to a small bowl and set aside.

Cook the pasta following the basic method (page 9), until al dente. Drain well and transfer to a large bowl. Add the tomato and olives, season generously with pepper, and cover to keep warm.

In a large skillet, heat the remaining 1 tablespoon oil over high heat. Add the onion, bell pepper, and anchovies, and cook, stirring, for 5 minutes, or until softened. Add the cucumber and cook, stirring, for 1 minute, or just until heated through. Stir in the lemon juice. Add to the pasta along with the mint-oregano oil, feta, and shredded mint, tossing until well combined. Transfer to a serving bowl and serve.

EGGPLANT-COUSCOUS TIMBALES

Serves   6

THIS DISH MAKES A LOVELY FIRST COURSE
OR LIGHT LUNCH. COUSCOUS AND GRILLED VEGETABLES
ARE SANDWICHED BETWEEN SLICES OF
TENDER GRILLED EGGPLANT IN RING MOLDS AND SERVED
WITH A SAFFRONY ROASTED PEPPER SAUCE.

3 orange, red, or yellow bell peppers

2 medium-size eggplants (about 1 pound each), peeled & cut into ¼-inch-thick slices

Olive oil

Salt & freshly ground pepper

1 medium-size zucchini, cut lengthwise into ¼-inch-thick slices

Two ¼-inch-thick slices red onion

1 tablespoon unsalted butter

1 cup couscous

2 cups chicken broth, preferably homemade (Winter, p. 11)

2 tablespoons golden raisins (optional)

Pinch of saffron threads

Pinch of sugar

Frisée or watercress, for garnish (optional)

Preheat a grill to high and brush with oil, or preheat the broiler.

Grill or broil the bell peppers, turning occasionally, for about 15 minutes, or until blackened on all sides. Remove the peppers to a plastic bag, seal tightly, and let steam for 10 minutes. When cool enough to handle, peel, core, and seed the peppers.

Meanwhile, lightly brush the eggplant slices with oil and season with salt and pepper. Grill or broil, turning occasionally, for about 15 minutes, or until very tender and dark brown. Transfer the eggplant to a large plate.

Brush the zucchini and onion with oil and season with salt and pepper. Grill or broil, turning them, for 8 minutes, or until tender. Cut the zucchini, onion, and 1 of the bell peppers into ¼-inch dice. Set aside.

Preheat the oven to 350°F.

In a small saucepan, melt the butter over medium-high heat. Add the couscous and cook, stirring, for 3 minutes, or until golden. Add 1¾ cups of the broth, the raisins, if using, and ½ teaspoon salt. Bring to a boil, cover, and remove from the heat. Let sit for 7 minutes. Transfer the couscous to a medium-size bowl and fluff with a fork. Add the zucchini, onion, and diced bell pepper, stirring to mix.

Grease six 3-inch-wide-x-2-inch-deep bottomless ring molds* and place on a nonstick baking sheet. Arrange half of the eggplant in the bottom of the molds, being sure not to leave any open spaces. Divide the couscous mixture evenly among the molds and cover with the remaining eggplant, pressing firmly to pack down the couscous. Bake the eggplant timbales for 10 minutes, or until heated through.

Meanwhile, prepare the bell pepper sauce: In a food processor or blender, combine the remaining 2 bell peppers, the remaining ¼ cup chicken broth, the saffron, and sugar, processing until smooth. Transfer to a small saucepan and season with salt and pepper. Keep the sauce warm over medium-low heat.

With a spatula, transfer the timbales to serving plates. Carefully lift off and remove the ring molds. Spoon some bell pepper sauce around each timbale, garnish with the frisée, if using, and serve.

*Bottomless ring molds are available in specialty cookware stores.

PENNETTE WITH BROCCOLI & OLIVES

Serves 4

THE COMBINATION OF OLIVES, GARLIC,
LEMON, AND BROCCOLI OFFERS A COMPLEXITY OF
FLAVORS WITHOUT BEING FUSSY OR
COMPLICATED. USE A MIX OF OIL-CURED AND BRINE-CURED
OLIVES, SUCH AS KALAMATA, GAETA,
PICHOLINE, SICILIAN, NIÇOISE AND/OR MOROCCAN.

1 large bunch broccoli, separated into 1-inch florets, stems trimmed, peeled & cut into ½-inch chunks

12 ounces pennette or mezzani

¼ cup extra-virgin olive oil

2 large garlic cloves, thinly sliced

⅛ teaspoon crushed red pepper flakes

Salt

1 cup chicken broth, preferably homemade (Winter, p. 11)

1 teaspoon grated lemon zest

½ cup pitted & coarsely chopped assorted olives

1 tablespoon fresh lemon juice

Freshly grated Pecorino Romano cheese, for serving

Bring a large pot of salted water to boil over high heat. Add the broccoli and cook for 5 minutes, or until crisp-tender. Using a slotted spoon, transfer the broccoli to a colander and set aside.

Cook the pasta in the broccoli water, following the basic method (page 9), until al dente. Drain the pasta, reserving ½ cup of the pasta water. Transfer the pasta to a large bowl and cover to keep warm.

In a large deep skillet, heat the oil over medium-high heat. Add the garlic and cook, stirring, for 30 seconds, or until softened. Add the broccoli and red pepper flakes, and season lightly with salt. Cook, stirring, for 2 minutes, or until the broccoli is browned around the edges. Stir in the broth and lemon zest and use a wooden spoon to mash half of the broccoli. Cook for 8 minutes, or until the liquid is evaporated and the broccoli is sizzling. Add the olives and lemon juice and cook for 1 minute, stirring.

Add the pasta and the reserved pasta water, and season lightly with salt. Cook for 1 to 2 minutes, or until most of the liquid is absorbed. Serve immediately in deep bowls, passing the Romano separately.

SPAGHETTI AGLIO OLIO WITH TOMATOES & BASIL

Serves 4

1 pound tomatoes, cut into ¼-inch dice

½ cup loosely packed shredded fresh basil

Salt & freshly ground pepper

12 ounces spaghetti or thin linguine

¼ cup fruity extra-virgin olive oil

3 large garlic cloves, thinly sliced

¼ cup freshly grated Asiago cheese

IN SUMMER, WHEN PRODUCE IS AT ITS BEST, I LIKE TO KEEP DISHES SIMPLE TO LET THE FLAVORS OF THE INGREDIENTS SHINE THROUGH. IN THIS VARIATION OF A CLASSIC UNCOOKED SUMMERTIME SAUCE, THE RAW RIPE TOMATOES ARE WARMED BY FRAGRANT GARLIC OIL AS WELL AS THE HOT PASTA.

In a large serving bowl, toss the tomatoes and basil together. Season with salt and a generous amount of pepper. Spread the tomatoes in an even layer in the bottom of the bowl.

Cook the spaghetti following the basic method (page 9), until al dente. Drain well and place on top of the tomatoes.

In a small skillet, heat the oil and garlic over medium-high heat. Cook, stirring, for 1 minute, or until the garlic is golden. Immediately pour over the pasta and toss until mixed well. Sprinkle with the Asiago and serve.

PASTA WITH ARTICHOKES & ALMONDS

Serves 4

TART LEMON AND SWEET ALMONDS MARRY WELL
WITH SMALL TENDER ARTICHOKES. BE SURE TO PEEL OFF
ALL OF THE TOUGH OUTER ARTICHOKE LEAVES,
LEAVING ONLY THE PALE YELLOW CONE IN THE CENTER.

5 tablespoons fresh lemon juice

2 pounds tiny artichokes (about 15)

12 ounces capellini

2 tablespoons extra-virgin olive oil

⅓ cup sliced unblanched almonds

3 large garlic cloves, thinly sliced

Salt & freshly ground pepper

3 tablespoons unsalted butter,
    cut into pieces

1 teaspoon chopped fresh lemon
    thyme, or shredded lemon
    balm (p. 11)

Parmesan cheese shavings (removed
    with a vegetable peeler),
    for garnish

Bring a large saucepan of water to a boil over high heat. Add 2 tablespoons of the lemon juice to a medium-size bowl of cold water. Meanwhile, peel back and snap off the tough outer leaves of the artichokes. Trim ½ inch off the tops. Cut the artichokes in half and then into thin wedges. Soak the artichokes in the lemon water for 1 minute.

Drain the artichokes, put into the boiling water, and cook for 3 minutes, until tender when pierced with a knife. Drain well and set aside.

Cook the capellini following the basic method (page 9), until al dente. Drain well, reserving ¼ cup of the pasta water. Transfer the pasta to a large serving bowl and cover to keep warm.

In a large skillet, heat the oil over high heat. Add the almonds and garlic and cook, stirring, for 2 minutes, or until golden. Transfer the almonds and garlic to a small bowl. Add the artichokes to the skillet, season with salt and pepper, and cook, stirring occasionally, for about 5 minutes, or just until golden. Add the remaining 3 tablespoons lemon juice, the butter, and the reserved pasta water to the skillet and bring to a boil.

Pour the sauce over the pasta. Add the almonds, garlic, and lemon thyme, and toss to combine. Transfer to a serving bowl, garnish with the Parmesan shavings, and serve.

PENNE WITH GOAT CHEESE & GARLIC CRUMBS

Serves 4

12 ounces penne

2 tablespoons plus 1 teaspoon
    unsalted butter

1 large garlic clove, minced

⅔ cup dried bread crumbs

1 tablespoon finely chopped
    fresh basil

Salt & freshly ground pepper

1 pound spinach, trimmed,
    washed & coarsely chopped

6 ounces goat cheese, crumbled
    (about 1½ cups)

2 tablespoons freshly grated
    Parmesan cheese

CRISP GOLDEN BREAD CRUMBS, TOASTED
WITH BUTTER, GARLIC, AND BASIL, ARE A FLAVORFUL
CONTRAST WITH PENNE, WILTED SPINACH, AND
CREAMY CHEVRE. TOSS THE INGREDIENTS TOGETHER JUST
BEFORE SERVING SO THE CRUMBS DON'T GET SOGGY.

Cook the penne following the basic method (page 9), until al dente. Drain, reserving ¼ cup of the pasta water. Transfer the pasta to a large bowl and cover to keep warm.

In a large deep skillet, melt 2 tablespoons of the butter over medium heat. Add the garlic and cook for 30 seconds, or until fragrant and just barely softened. Add the bread crumbs and cook, stirring, for about 2 minutes, or until light golden. Add the basil and cook for 2 minutes longer, or until the bread crumbs are deep golden. Transfer to a plate, season lightly with salt and pepper, and set aside.

Add the remaining 1 teaspoon butter to the skillet and melt over high heat. Add the spinach and cook, tossing, for 1 minute, or until wilted. Add the pasta and toss until well combined. Add the goat and Parmesan cheeses along with the reserved pasta water, and cook, stirring, for about 1 minute, or until the pasta is heated through and the goat cheese is softened. Transfer to a large serving bowl, sprinkle with the bread crumbs, and lightly toss. Serve immediately.

CAPELLINI WITH CUCUMBERS & SMOKED SALMON

Serves 4 to 6

FLAVORS PLAY WITH AND AGAINST EACH
OTHER IN THIS SIMPLE YET SOPHISTICATED DISH WHICH
RELIES ON VERY FEW INGREDIENTS.
THE SALTY SALMON IS BALANCED BY THE SWEET CORN,
CUCUMBER, AND TANGY CHAMPAGNE VINEGAR.

12 ounces capellini

3 tablespoons unsalted butter

2 large shallots, thinly sliced

2 large cucumbers, peeled, halved
    lengthwise, seeded & thinly
    sliced crosswise

2 ears fresh corn, kernels cut off

2 tablespoons vinegar, preferably
    champagne

¼ pound sliced smoked salmon

2 tablespoons snipped fresh chives

1 teaspoon shredded fresh
    lemon balm (p. 11)
    or lemon thyme leaves

2 tablespoons salmon roe,
    for garnish (optional)

Cook the capellini following the basic method (page 9), until al dente. Drain well, reserving a scant ¼ cup of the pasta water. Transfer the pasta to a large bowl and cover to keep warm.

In a large skillet, heat 1½ tablespoons of the butter over medium heat. Add the shallots and cook, stirring occasionally, for 5 minutes, or until softened. Add the cucumbers and corn and cook for 7 minutes, or until softened and just beginning to color. Add the vinegar, the remaining 1½ tablespoons butter, and the reserved pasta water, and bring to a boil over high heat. Add the pasta, salmon, and chives, tossing to combine. Cook, tossing, for 1 minute, or until the pasta has absorbed some of the liquid.

To serve, divide the pasta among heated bowls and garnish with the lemon balm and salmon roe, if using.

TUBETTINI WITH FAVA BEANS & MORELS

1¼ cups tubettini

1 pound fresh fava beans, shelled

¼ pound asparagus, tough ends removed

1 tablespoon extra-virgin olive oil

⅔ cup finely chopped onions

Scant ½ cup dried morels (¼ ounce), soaked in boiling water for 5 minutes, or until softened, then drained, or ¼ pound fresh morels, trimmed, briefly rinsed & thinly sliced

1½ cups vegetable broth

Salt & freshly ground white pepper

⅓ cup freshly grated Parmesan cheese

2 tablespoons unsalted butter, cut into pieces

2 tablespoons snipped fresh chives

> I LIKE TUBETTINI FOR THIS DISH BECAUSE IT STANDS UP TO VIGOROUS STIRRING WITHOUT FALLING APART AND THE LITTLE HOLLOW CENTERS TRAP THE BUTTERY SAUCE.

In a large saucepan of boiling salted water, cook the tubettini, stirring occasionally, for 4 minutes, or until barely al dente. Drain well and set aside.

Bring a medium-size saucepan of lightly salted water to a boil over high heat. Blanch the fava beans for 3 minutes. Transfer the fava beans to a colander and cool under cold running water. Drain and set aside.

Cook the asparagus in the same boiling water for 3 minutes, or just until tender. Drain and cool under cold water. Cut into 1-inch pieces and transfer to a small bowl. Slip the skins off the fava beans, add to the asparagus, and set aside.

In a medium-size saucepan, heat the oil over medium-high heat. Add the onions and cook, stirring, for 4 minutes, or until softened. Add the morels and cook, stirring, for 6 to 7 minutes, or until softened and just beginning to brown. Stir in the tubettini. Reduce the heat to medium-low and add ½ cup of the broth. Cook, stirring, for about 3 minutes, or until all the liquid is absorbed. Add the remaining 1 cup broth in 2 additions, cooking and stirring until the broth is absorbed and the pasta is al dente.

Stir in the fava beans and asparagus, and season with salt and pepper. Reduce the heat to low and cook to warm the vegetables through. Remove from the heat, stir in the Parmesan, butter, and chives, and serve.

LINGUINE WITH COCKLES

Serves 4

A SPICY TOMATO-AND-HOT-PEPPER-INFUSED
OIL ADDS HEAT AND DEPTH OF FLAVOR IN THIS UPDATED
VERSION OF THE SIMPLE CLASSIC LINGUINE
CON VONGOLE. COCKLES ARE SMALLER THAN CLAMS AND
HAVE A WONDERFULLY BRINY FLAVOR.

12 ounces thin linguine

3 tablespoons extra-virgin olive oil

2 tablespoons tomato paste

2 large garlic cloves, 1 minced
& 1 thinly sliced

¼ teaspoon crushed red pepper
flakes or more, to taste

Pinch of sugar

3 dozen cockles or 2 dozen
littleneck clams, scrubbed well

½ cup dry white wine

½ cup cold water

Salt

3 tablespoons finely chopped fresh
flat-leaf parsley

Cook the linguine following the basic method (page 9), or until barely al dente. Drain, transfer to a medium-size bowl, and cover to keep warm.

In a small skillet, combine the oil, tomato paste, minced garlic, red pepper flakes, and sugar. Cook over medium heat, stirring, for 2 minutes, or until fragrant and deep red. Pour through a strainer set over a small bowl, pressing on the solids with the back of a spoon. Discard the solids. In a large deep skillet, combine the cockles, wine, and water. Cover and cook over high heat for about 5 minutes, or until the cockles open. Remove the cockles from their shells, saving any juices; discard any that do not open. Transfer the cockles to a small bowl and cover to keep warm. Pour the cooking liquid and the clam juices through a paper towel–lined fine-mesh strainer set over a small bowl.

Wipe out the skillet. Add the hot pepper oil and sliced garlic to the pan and cook over medium heat for 2 minutes, or until the garlic is softened. Add the reserved clam liquid and bring to a boil. Add the pasta and cook, stirring, for 3 minutes, or until the pasta is al dente and most of the liquid is absorbed. Season with salt, if desired and stir in the cockles and parsley. Serve immediately in deep bowls.

PENNE WITH CHARRED PEPPERS & TUNA

¼ cup chopped fresh mint

2 teaspoons grated lemon zest

3 tablespoons extra-virgin olive oil

¾ pound tuna steak, about 1-inch thick, any dark meat removed

1 large red bell pepper, halved, cored, seeded & cut into ¼-inch-wide strips

1 large yellow bell pepper, halved, cored, seeded & cut into ¼-inch-wide strips

1 large Vidalia onion, thinly sliced

Salt & freshly ground pepper

12 ounces penne rigate

2 tablespoons sherry vinegar

1 tablespoon unsalted butter, cut into pieces

CHARRING THE TUNA GIVES IT A DELICIOUS SMOKY QUALITY WHICH IS AN ENTICING CONTRAST TO THE DELICATE TASTE AND TENDER TEXTURE OF THE TUNA.

In a small dish combine the mint, lemon zest, and 1 tablespoon of the oil. Rub the tuna with the mint-oil mixture, then cover and refrigerate.

Heat a large cast-iron skillet over high heat. Add 1 tablespoon of the oil to the skillet. Add the bell peppers and cook, stirring, for 3 minutes, or until softened. Add the onion, season with salt and pepper, and cook, stirring, for about 4 minutes longer, or until the vegetables are lightly charred. Transfer the vegetables to a large bowl and cover. Set the skillet aside.

Cook the penne following the basic method (page 9), until al dente. Drain well, reserving ¼ cup of the pasta water. Transfer the pasta to a separate large bowl and cover to keep warm.

Return the skillet to high heat and add the remaining 1 tablespoon oil. Scrape most of the marinade off the tuna and reserve. Season the tuna with salt and pepper. Cook for 2 minutes on each side for medium-rare, or to the desired degree of doneness. Transfer to a cutting board, cover, and let rest for 5 minutes. Cut into ¼-inch-thick slices and cover.

Meanwhile, return the skillet to high heat. Add the vegetables, the reserved marinade, the vinegar, and the reserved pasta water. Bring to a boil over high heat, season with salt and pepper, and swirl in the butter. Add to the pasta, tossing until the butter is melted. To serve, divide the pasta among serving plates and top with the sliced tuna.

SPAGHETTI WITH WATERCRESS & SMOKED TROUT

Serves 4

1 pound spaghetti

¼ cup extra-virgin olive oil

1 bunch watercress, stems trimmed
& chopped, leaves reserved

2 large garlic cloves, thinly sliced

⅛ teaspoon crushed red pepper
flakes, or to taste

1 whole smoked trout (about ½
pound), boned, skinned & flaked

1 teaspoon grated lemon zest

Salt

1 tablespoon fresh lemon juice

Freshly grated Parmesan cheese,
for serving

IF SMOKED TROUT ISN'T AVAILABLE, ONE CUP SHREDDED GOOD-QUALITY SMOKED TURKEY, CHICKEN, OR WHITING CAN BE SUBSTITUTED IN THIS ELEGANT DISH WITH EQUALLY DELICIOUS RESULTS.

Cook the spaghetti following the basic method (page 9), until al dente. Drain, transfer to a large serving bowl, and cover to keep warm.

In a large skillet, heat the oil over medium heat. Add the watercress stems and cook, stirring, for 2 minutes, or until softened. Add the garlic and red pepper flakes and cook for 1 minute, until the garlic is golden. Add the watercress leaves, trout, and lemon zest. Season lightly with salt and cook, stirring, for 1 minute, or until the leaves are just wilted.

Pour the sauce over the pasta, add the lemon juice, and toss. Transfer to a serving bowl and serve, passing the Parmesan on the side.

TOASTED COUSCOUS WITH RATATOUILLE

Serves 4

TOASTING COUSCOUS GIVES IT A NUTTY QUALITY. HERE, MIXED WITH SUNFLOWER SEEDS AND SWEET CURRANTS, AND SERVED WITH SUMMER'S BEST RATATOUILLE, IT MAKES A PERFECT HOT-WEATHER MEAL FOR VEGETARIANS AND NON-VEGETARIANS ALIKE.

RATATOUILLE

3 tablespoons olive oil

2 red or yellow bell peppers, halved, cored, seeded & cut into ¾-inch pieces

1 large onion, chopped

1 large garlic clove, minced

1 small eggplant (about ¾ pound), peeled & cut into ¾-inch cubes

1 each medium-size zucchini & yellow squash, cut into ¾-inch cubes

3 medium-size tomatoes, peeled (p. 6), seeded & cut into ¾-inch chunks, juice reserved

Pinch of sugar

Salt & freshly ground pepper

2 tablespoons unsalted butter

1 small onion, finely chopped

1 cup couscous

1¾ cups chicken broth, preferably homemade (Winter, p. 11)

¼ cup currants

Salt

¼ cup sunflower seeds, toasted

Prepare the ratatouille: In a large saucepan, heat the oil over medium-high heat. Add the bell peppers, onion, and garlic and cook, stirring occasionally, for 8 minutes, or until softened and lightly golden. Add the eggplant, zucchini, and yellow squash and cook, stirring, for 7 to 8 minutes, or until lightly golden and crisp-tender. Add the tomatoes and their juice, the sugar, and a pinch each of salt and pepper. Cook over medium heat, stirring occasionally, for 18 to 20 minutes, or until the vegetables are tender and the sauce is slightly thickened. Season with additional salt and pepper, remove from the heat, and cover to keep warm.

Meanwhile, in a medium-size saucepan, melt the butter over medium-high heat. Add the onion and cook, stirring occasionally, for 4 minutes, or until softened. Add the couscous and cook, stirring constantly, for about 3 minutes, or until fragrant and toasted. Stir in the broth and currants, season with salt, and bring to a boil. Cover the pan, remove from the heat, and let sit for about 7 minutes, or until the liquid is absorbed.

To serve, fluff the couscous with a fork and stir in the sunflower seeds. Divide among large shallow bowls, spoon the ratatouille over, and serve immediately.

VEGETABLE RIBBONS WITH CRÈME FRAÎCHE

Serves 4

LIKE THE PAPPARDELLE NOODLES THEY MIRROR, THESE TENDER YOUNG VEGETABLE RIBBONS TRAP THE DELICIOUSLY SWEET CREAMY SAUCE IN THEIR FOLDS.

1¼ pounds boneless skinless chicken breast halves

1½ tablespoons extra-virgin olive oil

1 teaspoon grated lemon zest

Freshly ground pepper

4 fresh thyme sprigs

2 small yellow squash, cut lengthwise into ⅛-inch-thick slices

2 small zucchini, cut lengthwise into ⅛-inch-thick slices

2 medium-size carrots, cut lengthwise into ⅛-inch-thick slices

12 ounces pappardelle

Salt

2 large shallots, thinly sliced

¼ cup plus 2 tablespoons crème fraîche

1 teaspoon fresh lemon juice

Pound the chicken to ¼-inch thickness. Rub with 1½ teaspoons of the oil, sprinkle with ½ teaspoon of the lemon zest, and season with pepper. Put a thyme sprig on each breast, cover, and refrigerate for 15 minutes.

Meanwhile, bring a medium-size saucepan of lightly salted water to a boil over high heat. Add the squash, zucchini, and carrots and cook, for about 2 minutes, or until just wilted. Drain and set aside.

Cook the pappardelle following the basic method (page 9), until al dente. Drain well. Transfer the pasta to a large bowl and cover.

Heat a large nonstick skillet over high heat. Season the chicken with salt and cook for about 2 minutes on each side, or until cooked through. Transfer to a cutting board. Slice the chicken into long strips. Remove the leaves from 2 of the thyme sprigs and chop. Discard the remaining sprigs.

Return the skillet to high heat. Add the remaining 1 tablespoon oil and the shallots and cook, stirring, for 3 minutes, or until the shallots are softened. Add the reserved vegetables, season with salt and pepper, and cook, stirring, for 2 to 3 minutes, or just until brown along the edges. Add the chicken, along with any accumulated juices, the thyme, and pasta and cook, gently tossing, until heated through. Remove from the heat and stir in the crème fraîche, lemon juice, and the remaining ½ teaspoon lemon zest. Season with salt and pepper, toss, and transfer to a serving bowl.

GRILLED VEGETABLES WITH GARLIC CREAM

Serves 4 to 6

½ pound baby carrots

4 large garlic cloves, lightly smashed

2 pounds assorted baby squash, such as pattypan, zucchini, and/or yellow

2 tablespoons chopped mixed fresh herbs, such as oregano, thyme & basil

2 tablespoons canola or other vegetable oil

Salt & freshly ground pepper

1 tablespoon unsalted butter

¾ cup heavy cream

Small pinch of freshly grated nutmeg

12 ounces rigatoni

Freshly grated Asiago or Parmesan cheese, for serving

USE A VEGETABLE GRILL RACK THAT SITS DIRECTLY ON THE GRILL FOR THIS RECIPE. THE VEGETABLES WON'T SLIP THROUGH THE GRATE, SO YOU WON'T NEED TO WATCH QUITE SO DILIGENTLY.

Bring a small saucepan of water to a boil over high heat. Add the carrots and garlic and cook for 3 minutes, or until the carrots are crisp-tender. Drain and set the garlic aside in a small dish.

In a large bowl, combine the carrots, squash, herbs, and oil. Season with salt and a generous amount of pepper and let sit for 20 minutes.

Preheat a grill to medium and brush with oil, or preheat the broiler.

Grill or broil the vegetables, turning occasionally, for 15 minutes, or until tender and dark golden. Transfer to a large serving bowl and cover.

In a small saucepan, melt the butter over medium heat. Add the reserved garlic and cook, stirring, for 3 to 4 minutes, or until golden and tender. Remove from the heat. Using a fork, mash the garlic into a paste. Return to the heat, add the cream, and bring to a boil. Cook for 5 minutes, or until slightly reduced and thickened. Season with salt and pepper and add the nutmeg. Keep warm over very low heat.

Cook the rigatoni following the basic method (page 9), until al dente. Drain well and add along with the garlic cream to the vegetables, tossing until mixed well. To serve, divide the pasta among large shallow bowls and sprinkle with the Asiago.

PASTA WITH GORGONZOLA DOLCE

Serves 4 to 6

SWEET GORGONZOLA, *GORGONZOLA DOLCE*, IS
ITALY'S PREMIER BLUE CHEESE. THIS SOFT, MILD-FLAVORED
BLUE-VEINED GORGONZOLA IS DELICATE
ENOUGH TO SERVE AS AN APPETIZER OR EVEN AS PART
OF A DESSERT. HERE, IT PAIRS PERFECTLY
WITH THE SLIGHT SALTINESS OF THE PROSCIUTTO.

1 pound linguine

1 tablespoon extra-virgin olive oil

2 medium-size shallots, thinly sliced

¼-inch-thick slice prosciutto (about 4 ounces), cut into 3-x-¼-inch strips

½ cup oil-packed sun-dried tomatoes, chopped

Crushed red pepper flakes

Salt & freshly ground pepper

½ cup chicken broth, preferably homemade (Winter, p.11)

4 ounces imported Gorgonzola dolce cheese, crumbled (1 cup)

2 tablespoons chopped fresh flat-leaf parsley

Cook the linguine following the basic method (page 9), until al dente. Drain well, reserving ¼ cup of the pasta water. Transfer the pasta to a large serving bowl and cover to keep warm.

In a large nonreactive skillet, heat the oil over medium-high heat. Add the shallots and cook, stirring, for 1 minute. Add the prosciutto and sun-dried tomatoes, season with red pepper flakes, salt, and pepper, and cook, stirring, for 5 minutes, or until the prosciutto is lightly browned. Add the broth, bring to a boil, and cook for 3 to 4 minutes, or until the liquid is slightly reduced.

Add to the pasta along with the Gorgonzola and parsley, toss well, and serve in large shallow bowls.

SEAFOOD PAELLA

LOBSTER STOCK

2 live lobsters (1 to 1¼
    pounds each)

2 tablespoons tomato paste

¼ cup brandy

10 cups cold water

1 medium-size onion, quartered

5 each fresh flat-leaf parsley
    & thyme sprigs

¼ teaspoon saffron threads

1 bay leaf

PAELLA

1 tablespoon olive oil

1 medium-size onion,
    finely chopped

1 large garlic clove, minced

2 ounces Serrano ham, prosciutto,
    or Westphalian ham, cut into
    ¼-inch dice

1 cup orzo

1 large red bell pepper, roasted
    (p. 22), peeled, cored, seeded
    & cut into ¼-inch-wide strips

1 medium-size tomato, coarsely
    chopped

Salt & freshly ground pepper

PAELLA IS A CLASSIC SPANISH DISH THAT OFTEN FEATURES SEAFOOD, CHICKEN, HAM, SAUSAGE, AND TOMATO WITH SAFFRON-SCENTED RICE. HERE, I'VE USED ORZO INSTEAD OF THE MORE DIFFICULT-TO-FIND MEDIUM-GRAIN VALENCIA RICE.

Prepare the lobster stock: Bring a large heavy-bottomed pot of water to a rolling boil over high heat. Plunge the lobsters head first into the boiling water and cook for 3 minutes, or just until red. Remove the lobsters and cool under cold running water; drain well. Twist off and remove the claws and tails. With a large knife or cleaver, cut each tail into 3 pieces. Using a lobster cracker, crack the claws. Set aside.

Wipe out the pot. Break the lobster bodies into 2-inch pieces. Put into the pot along with the tomato paste and cook, uncovered, over high heat, stirring often, for 3 to 5 minutes, or until the tomato paste looks sandy. Sprinkle with the brandy and standing back, ignite with a long match. Let the flames subside. Add the water, onion, parsley, thyme, saffron, and bay leaf to the pot and bring to a boil. Reduce the heat to medium and simmer, covered, for 1 hour.

Pour the strained stock through a large strainer set over a large bowl. Wipe out the pot, return the stock to the pot, and boil, uncovered, over high heat, for 6 to 8 minutes, or until reduced to 5 cups. Set aside.

Prepare the paella: In a large nonstick skillet with a tight-fitting lid, heat the oil over medium heat. Add the onion and garlic and cook,

6 littleneck clams, scrubbed well

6 mussels, debearded &
  scrubbed well

1 pound fresh peas, shelled,
  or ½ cup frozen peas, thawed

¼ pound Italian Romano beans,
  cut into 1-inch pieces

covered, for 5 to 7 minutes, or until softened and golden. Add the ham and cook, stirring, for 3 minutes, or until lightly browned around the edges. Add the orzo and cook, stirring, for 4 minutes, or until golden. Stir in the bell pepper, tomato, 2 cups of the reserved stock, and season lightly with salt and pepper. (Refrigerate or freeze the remaining stock for another use.) Cover the skillet and cook for 7 minutes. Add the reserved lobster, the clams, mussels, peas, and green beans. Cover and cook, stirring occasionally, for 12 minutes, or until the clams and mussels open and the orzo is al dente. Remove from the heat and let sit, covered, for 5 minutes. Discard any unopened shellfish and serve directly from the skillet.

FARFALLE WITH GRILLED SWORDFISH

Serves 4

Smoky grilled swordfish and
yellow pear tomatoes are tossed with
delicate butterfly-shaped pasta
and a richly flavored balsamic vinegar and
tomato butter sauce. With
so many varieties of tomatoes available,
feel free to experiment,
using a mix of colors and shapes.

1 carrot, finely chopped

1 large shallot, chopped

1½ tablespoons tomato paste

½ teaspoon chopped fresh
rosemary

1 tablespoon sugar

1 cup cold water

¼ cup balsamic vinegar

2 tablespoons unsalted butter,
cut into pieces

Salt & freshly ground pepper

12 ounces farfalle

1 pound swordfish steak, 1-inch
thick, cut into cubes

2 tablespoons olive oil

24 tiny yellow pear or cherry
tomatoes

Preheat a grill to high and brush with oil, or place a stovetop grill pan over medium-high heat. Soak eight 8- to 10-inch bamboo skewers in cold water for at least 30 minutes.

In a medium-size saucepan, combine the carrot, shallot, tomato paste, rosemary, sugar, water, and vinegar. Cook over medium heat, stirring occasionally, for 15 minutes, or until the vegetables are softened and most of the liquid has evaporated.

Press the liquid through a fine-mesh strainer set over a medium-size bowl, pressing on the solids with the back of a wooden spoon to extract all the liquid; discard the solids. Wipe out the saucepan and return the liquid to the pan. Cook over medium-high heat until reduced to ½ cup. Remove from the heat and gradually whisk in the butter. Season with salt and pepper and cover to keep warm.

Cook the farfalle following the basic method (page 9), until al dente. Drain, transfer to a large serving bowl, and cover to keep warm.

Put the swordfish onto 4 of the skewers. Brush generously with the oil and season with salt and pepper. Put the cherry tomatoes on the remaining 4 skewers. Grill the swordfish and tomatoes, turning once, for about 2 minutes on each side, or until the swordfish is cooked through and the tomatoes are softened and blistered.

Remove the swordfish and tomatoes from the skewers and add to the pasta along with the reserved sauce. Gently toss to combine, season with salt and pepper, and serve hot.

WEIGHTS

Ounces and Pounds	Metric Equivalent
1/4 ounce	7 grams
1/3 ounce	10 g
1/2 ounce	14 g
1 ounce	28 g
1 1/2 ounces	42 g
1 3/4 ounces	50 g
2 ounces	57 g
3 ounces	85 g
3 1/2 ounces	100 g
4 ounces (1/4 pound)	114 g
6 ounces	170 g
8 ounces (1/2 pound)	227 g
9 ounces	250 g
16 ounces (1 pound)	464 g

TEMPERATURE

°F (Fahrenheit)	°C (Centigrade or Celsius)
32 (water freezes)	0
200	95
212 (water boils)	100
250	120
275	135
300 (slow oven)	150
325	160
350 (moderate oven)	175
375	190
400 (hot oven)	205
425	220
450 (very hot oven)	232
475	245
500 (extremely hot oven)	260

LIQUID MEASURES

tsp.: teaspoon / Tbs.: tablespoon

Spoons and Cups	Metric Equivalents
1/4 tsp.	1.23 milliliters
1/2 tsp.	2.5 ml
3/4 tsp.	3.7 ml
1 tsp.	5 ml
1 dessertspoon	10 ml
1 Tbs. (3 tsp.)	15 ml
2 Tbs. (1 ounce)	30 ml
1/4 cup	60 ml
1/3 cup	80 ml
1/2 cup	120 ml
2/3 cup	160 ml
3/4 cup	180 ml
1 cup (8 ounces)	240 ml
2 cups (1 pint)	480 ml
3 cups	720 ml
4 cups (1 quart)	1 liter
4 quarts (1 gallon)	3.75 liters

LENGTH

U.S. Measurements	Metric Equivalent
1/8 inch	3 mm
1/4 inch	6 mm
3/8 inch	1 cm
1/2 inch	1.2 cm
3/4 inch	2 cm
1 inch	2.5 cm
1 1/4 inches	3.1 cm
1 1/2 inches	3.7 cm
2 inches	5 cm
3 inches	7.5 cm
4 inches	10 cm
5 inches	12.5 cm

APPROXIMATE EQUIVALENTS

1 kilo is slightly more than 2 pounds
1 liter is slightly more than 1 quart
1 meter is slightly over 3 feet
1 centimeter is approximately 3/8 inch

SUMMER

PASTA

INDEX

Almond Anise Aglio Olio	13
Capellini with Cucumbers & Smoked Salmon	37
Eggplant-Couscous Timbales	31
Farfalle with Grilled Swordfish	51
Farfallini & Chicken with Chive Dressing	23
Fusilli con Sugo Francesca	9
Greek Salad with Pasta & Mint	29
Grilled Salmon & Pasta Salad	26
Grilled Seafood Pasta Salad	24
Grilled Vegetables with Garlic Cream	46
Lamb & Acini De Pepe Tabbouleh	28
Linguine & Pesto Genovese	14
Linguine with Cockles	39
Linguine with Lemon Walnut Pesto	11
Linguine with Smoky Tomato Coulis	8
Lobster & Fresh Corn Salad	27
Orecchiette Giardinere	18
Orzo Salad with Peppers & Asparagus	22
Panzanella with Pennette	21
Pasta with Artichokes & Almonds	35
Pasta with Gorgonzola Dolce	47
Pasta with Olive-Caper Pesto	16
Pasta with Oven-Dried Tomato Tapenade	6
Penne with Charred Peppers & Tuna	40
Penne with Goat Cheese & Garlic Crumbs	36
Penne with Summer Arrabbiata	10
Pennette with Broccoli & Olives	33
Seafood Paella	48
Spaghetti Aglio Olio with Tomatoes & Basil	34
Spaghetti with Salsina Verde	15
Spaghetti with Watercress & Smoked Trout	42
Toasted Couscous with Ratatouille	43
Tomato-Mozzarella Salad with Pasta	17
Tubettini with Fava Beans & Morels	38
Vegetable Ribbons with Crème Fraîche	45